G H

JOSHUA SOBOL

Joshua Sobol was born in 1939 in Israel. He studied in Paris at the Sorbonne where he received a degree in Philosophy. Returning to Israel, he taught aesthetics and directed many workshops at Tel Aviv University, Seminar Hakibbutzim and Beit Tzvi Drama Schools. Most of his plays have been premiered at the Haifa Municipal Theatre, where he worked as Artistic Director from 1984. These include: *The Days to Come, Status Quo Vadis, New Year's Eve '72, The Joker, The Night of the Twentieth, Nerves, The Tenants, Gog and Magog Show, Soul of a Jew, Ghetto, Shooting Magda (The Palestinian Girl)*.

Sobol has also written for other theatres in Israel. These plays include: *Repentance, Passodoble, Homeward Angel, Wedding Night, Wars of the Jews, The Last of the Workers*.

Soul of a Jew was seen at the 1983 Edinburgh Festival, and in 1985 both *Soul of a Jew* and *Ghetto* were staged at the Berlin Festival followed by performances thoughout Germany. Sobol's plays have been produced all over the world in many languages.

DAVID LAN

David Lan's plays include two short works, *Painting a Wall* and *Red Earth*; a trilogy consisting of *The Winter Dancers, Sergeant Ola* and *Desire; Flight* and *A Mouthful of Birds*, a collaboration with Caryl Churchill. He has written two films for TV, *The Sunday Judge* and *The Crossing*, and, with Judd Ne'eman, a feature *Streets of Yesterday*. He has also published an anthropological study *Guns and Rain: Guerillas and Spirit Mediums in Zimbabwe*.

Front cover illustration designed by Tim Moore

JOSHUA SOBOL

GHETTO

In a version by David Lan
with lyrics translated
and music arranged by Jeremy Sams

N
H
B

NICK HERN BOOKS

A division of Walker Books Limited

A Nick Hern Book

Joshua Sobol's *Ghetto* in a version by David Lan first published in Great Britain in 1989 as an original paperback by Nick Hern Books, 87 Vauxhall Walk, London SE11 5HJ

This version was prepared from a literal translation from the original Hebrew by Miriam Shlesinger, published by the Institute for the Translation of Hebrew Literature. Some scenes have been rewritten by Joshua Sobol especially for this version
Copyright in this version © 1989 by Joshua Sobol and David Lan
Lyrics and music by inhabitants of the Vilna Ghetto translated and arranged by Jeremy Sams: translation and arrangements © 1989 Jeremy Sams
Extracts from *Ghetto in Flames* by permission of Holocaust Library, New York. Copyright © 1982 by Yitzhak Arab and Yad Vashem.
Extracts from *The Cultural Life of the Vilna Ghetto* from the *Simon Wiesenthal Center Annual, Volume I* © Solon Beinfeld. Extracts from *The Diary of the Vilna Ghetto* from *Volume XIII of YIVO Annual of Jewish Social Science*, by permission. Copyright © 1965 YIVO Institute for Jewish Research, New York
Map of Vilna © Martin Gilbert

Set in Baskerville by BookEns, Saffron Walden, Essex
Printed by Billings & Sons, Worcester

British Library Cataloguing in Publication Data
    Lan, David. 1952–
      Ghetto.
      I. Title II Sobol, Joshua, Ghetto.
      822'914
      ISBN 1 85459 021 9

Caution
All rights whatsoever in this play are strictly reserved. Requests to reproduce the text in whole or in part should be addressed to the publisher. Application for performance in any medium or for translation into any language should be addressed to the author's sole agent, Margaret Ramsay Ltd, 14a Goodwin's Court, St Martin's Lane, London WC2N 4LL. No performance may be given unless a licence has been obtained prior to rehearsal. Requests for licence to perform this arrangement of the songs and music should be addressed to Jeremy Sams c/o The National Theatre, South Bank, London SE1 9PX

CONTENTS

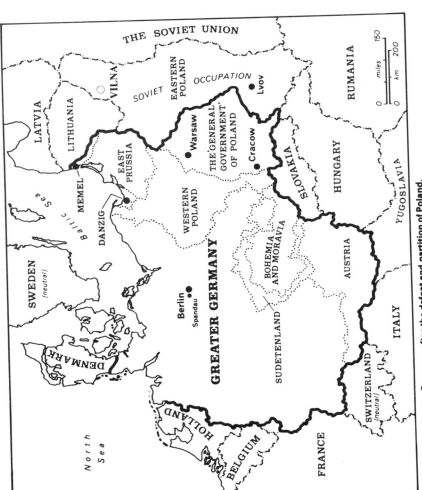

The borders of Greater Germany after the defeat and partition of Poland.

Chronology of Events in Vilna
1939–1943

1939

September	1	Germany invades Poland.
	19	Soviets occupy Vilna as a result of the German-Soviet Non-Aggression Pact.
October	28	Lithuania takes Vilna over from the Soviet Union: hundreds of Jews flee towards the U.S.S.R. In the next five years only 75,000 Jews emigrate to Palestine as against the 256,000 in the years 1932–9.

1940

Vilna's population according to Lithuanian figures:

Total population:	200,000
Jews:	80,000
Lithuanians:	60,000
Poles and others:	60,000

February	28	Emigration to Palestine forbidden

1941

June	22	Germany invades the U.S.S.R.; air-raids on Vilna; several thousand Jews leave the city. Kruk starts his diary.
	24	German troops march into Vilna; the majority of Jewish fugitives are killed, many are forced back into the city, fewer than 3000 get away; the Lithuanian police comes under German command.
July	2	Einsatzkommando 9 (Death Squad 9) arrives in Vilna.
	3	Jews in Vilna are ordered to wear a yellow star and obey a curfew from 6 p.m. to 6 a.m.

	4	Foundation of the Judenrat (Jewish Council) by order of the German military authorities.
	4–20	5,000 Jews murdered by EK9 in Ponar, just outside Vilna.
	8	Jews are banned from the main street of Vilna
August	1	The German military authorities hand over power to a German civil administration.
	9	EK3 takes over from EK9.
September	2	3,700 Jews (among them the complete Judenrat) are shot by way of reprisal for an alleged Jewish assassination attempt on 31 August.
	6	The Germans designate seventeen – later only seven – streets as the Jewish ghetto. Vilna's Jewry is driven into this ghetto, which is under the command of SS officer Franz Maurer.
	7	A five-man Judenrat is set up. Gens becomes chief of the (Jewish) ghetto police.
	8	Opening of the library.
	12	Mass-murder of 3,334 Vilna Jews in Ponar.
October	1	Yom Kippur 'Action': 3,700 Jews are taken away.
	3–21	6,496 Jew are killed in three separate 'actions'.
	13	Confiscation of all Jewish property.
October		3,000 work-passes are distributed.
October December	24–22	7,110 Jews without work-passes are shot.

November	27	The Judenrat resolves to protect the cultural life and artefacts of the ghetto.

1942

January	18	A writers and artists association is set up. The first public symphony concert takes place.
	20	The Wannsee (Berlin) Conference on the Final Solution of the Jewish Question: plans include the decimation of the Jews through forced labour with insufficient nourishment.
	21	Foundation of the F.P.O. (United Partisan Organisation) dedicated to armed resistance and sabotage.
February	5	Geburtenverbot (a ban on giving birth) is introduced for Jews.
	10	Foundation of a musicians association.
April	14	The police order official registration of all musical instruments in the ghetto.
	26	First performance in the Ghetto Theatre. Quarrel between Gens and Weiskopf about ethics of producing goods for the Germans.
May	2	Germany launches her summer offensive on the Soviet Union.
July	11	Maurer appoints Gens leader of the ghetto. His deputies are Anatol Fried (administration) and Salk Dessler (police).
	26	84 elderly Jews are handed over to the Lithuanian police. A literature prize for plays about the ghetto is announced.
October		A Polish underground newspaper publishes population figures for Vilna in 1942 (cf. 1940):

Total population:	142,000
Jews	12,000
Lithuanians	33,000
Poles	97,000

November		Premiere of *The Man under the Bridge* in the Ghetto Theatre.
December	13	Celebration on the occasion of the 100,000th book borrowed from the library.
1943 March	25	Five smaller ghettos in towns around Vilna are liquidated.
	27	Premiere of *The Treasure* by David Pinski.
April	5	4,000 Jews from the smaller ghettos are shot in Ponar.
May	5	Beginning of a mass exodus from the ghetto.
	14	Almost all the entrances to the ghetto are walled up.
	15	Gens speaks out against the keeping of arms in the ghetto.
June		Weiskopf is shot. Premiere of the revue, *Peshe from Rzesza*. Hans Kittel becomes officer responsible for the Security Police for Jewish Affairs in Vilna.
	10	Premiere of the ghetto's first Hebrew play, *The Eternal Jew* by David Pinski.
	12	Gens shoots a youth at the ghetto gate who has himself shot a policeman in an attempt to flee the ghetto.
	26	Uprising against the ghetto police.

	27	Dessler dismisses the 11 policemen, who are members of or sympathisers with the F.P.O.
July	14	Last entry in Kruk's diary.
	16	Jewish workers with jobs outside the ghetto are dismissed. Transportation to the concentration camps begins.
September		Rehearsals of *Tevye the Milkman* by Sholem Aleichem.
	1	The German authorities demand 5,000 Jews for transportation. In the course of an armed uprising in the ghetto, several members of the F.P.O. are arrested.
	2	Gens sets up an auxiliary police force, selects 5,000 people and hands them over to the authorities.
	7	The F.P.O. retreat into the woods.
	14	Gens is arrested and shot, ignoring earlier warnings to escape.
September	15	Kittel names Dessler as Gens's successor.
	18	Dessler flees. Kittel names a new Police Chief.
	23	The Vilna Ghetto, comprising about 10,000 Jews, is liquidated.
1944 July	7	The Soviets reach Vilna.

Vilna: the 'Jerusalem of Lithuania'

[Extracts from the Foreword to *Ghetto in Flames* by Yitzhak Arad, Holocaust Library, New York 1982]

From the end of the fifteenth century a large and flourishing community existed in Vilna. The large number of rabbinic scholars, writers, and centres of learning and Torah studies in Vilna assured the city a central place in the cultural life of Lithuanian Jewry. In the Jewish world at large Vilna was known as 'Jerusalem of Lithuania'.

Throughout her history Vilna was ruled successively by the Lithuanians, the Poles, the Russians, and, during World War I, even the Germans. Between the two world wars Vilna was under Polish domination. The Polish Government conducted a policy of 'Polonization' of the city and surrounding area. The Poles ousted the Jews from a variety of economic footholds, both in industry and commerce, and, as a result, the Jews' economic position deteriorated.

In contrast to the economic decline of Vilna Jewry, a lively and flourishing cultural life developed. Zionist, religious, and Yiddishist groups were active in preserving the Jewish character of the community and in fostering Jewish consciousness through the network of educational and cultural establishments. The great majority of Jewish children were educated in elementary schools in which the language of instruction was Yiddish or Hebrew . . .

Vilna Jewry had many institutions in which the treasures of Jewish culture found their repository. Prominent among the large libraries was 'Strashun', founded in 1893, which contained some 35,000 volumes: half the collection was rabinical literature. It also possessed manuscripts dating to the fifteenth century. The Jewish Historical and Ethnographical Society, established in 1903, collected rare Jewish material in the fields of history, folklore, literature, drama, music, and art. Its library preserved original Yiddish and Hebrew manuscripts by renowned authors. The Jewish Scientific Institute, YIVO (Yiddisher Visnshaftlecher Institut), founded in 1924, dealt in the collection of cultural riches and in research work. YIVO possessed a collection of about 20,000 books, Yiddish newspapers published in all parts of the world, and rare paintings and musical compositions by Jewish artists. Several Jewish publishing houses were active in the city, and five daily newspapers and periodicals were published regularly . . .

During the final years of Polish rule, anti-Semitism and discrimination against the Jews became rampant in all spheres of life and assumed a violent form. Jews were attacked, and a bomb exploded in a synagogue at the beginning of February 1935. The anti-Jewish campaign was particularly rife on the University of Vilna campus. Separate seating for Jewish students, on the left side of the classrooms, was introduced in all universities in Poland in the fall of 1937. Mounting anti-Semitism and discriminatory practices continued almost until the very outbreak of the Germano-Polish war on September 1, 1939.

During the year of Soviet rule in Vilna, between June 1940 and June 1941, all Jewish organizations and institutions were disbanded. Therefore, when the Germans invaded the U.S.S.R. there was no recognized Jewish organization to deal with them . . .

During the Holocaust the Jews of Vilna endured most of the edicts and persecutions that the Germans inflicted upon Jewry at large – expropriation of property, wearing the yellow badge, forced labour, abductions, humiliation and massacre by the Einsatzgruppen (Death Squads), confinement within the ghetto, deportations to forced-labour and death-camps. Faced with these eventualities, their problem was how to organize, how to conduct themselves, in order to survive.

The operating forces in the 'Jewish Street' were the Judenrat (Jewish Council) and its institutions, existing political groups as well as those that came into being in the wake of ghetto conditions, the armed underground, and the Jewish public as a whole. The community suddenly found itself isolated from the rest of the Jewish world, a world with which it had, in the past, formed close ties and into which it was completely integrated. Its relationship with the non-Jewish environment, in whose midst it had existed for many generations, was radically transformed. In spite of the fact that, even in the past, the Jews had endured enmity and much suffering at the hands of the local population, the eruption of savage, unrestrained hatred during the Nazi period came as a shock. The Jews were compelled to establish relations with an alien and hostile government that regarded them as subhuman and fit only for exploitation and extermination. The human values in which they believed and on which they had built their lives tottered and collapsed.

In this cruel reality, Vilna Jewry struggled to survive and seek rescue. The daily struggle was for life itself, to survive in the face of hunger and disease. Jewish Vilna embodied the majority of hardships and torment that European Jewry at large underwent during the Holocaust, and its responses sum up most of the options that were available to the Jews during this tragic epoch. Vilna Jewry was a microcosm of the fate of all Jewish communities in Eastern Europe.

The Process of Extermination

[Extracted from *Ghetto in Flames* by Yitzhak Arad, Holocaust Library, New York, 1982]

Einsatzkommando 9 [Death Squad 9] crossed the old border of the Reich en route to Vilna on July 1, 1941, and arrived in the city the following day. The first two days, July 2 and 3, were devoted to familiarizing themselves with the conditions and arrangements for the extermination actions.

The murder of small groups of Jews by the Lithuanians had already begun before the arrival of E.K.9. The Lithuanians seized Jews on the streets and killed them in the forest near Ponar. The information was helpful to E.K.9 because Ponar could be used for mass murder, and the Lithuanians could be helpful in the murder actions. This enabled E.K.9 to launch the extermination campaign without delay and on a large scale.

The Einsatzkommando completed its organization in Vilna, and on July 4, 1941, began its massacres. The number of victims mounted daily.

The process of extermination carried out by E.K.9 was conducted in three simultaneous and successive stages:

> Stage I: Kidnapping Jews from the streets and from their homes and concentrating them in the Lukiszki prison.
> Stage II: Detention of the victims in prison as a transit station to Ponar.
> Stage III: Transporting the Jews from Lukiszki to Ponar and murdering them there.

The problem of manpower needed to discharge the functions of extermination on such a large scale was solved by incorporating Lithuanian police and other units in the E.K.9 actions. Einsatzgruppen report No. 17 of July 9 referred to 'units of the Lithuanian police subordinate to E.K.9.' Einsatzgruppen Report No. 21 of July 13 stated:

> In Vilna . . . the Lithuanian *Ordnungspolizei*, which was placed under the command of the Einsatzkommando after the disbandment of the Lithuanian political police, received

instructions to take part in the Jewish extermination actions. Consequently, 150 Lithuanians are engaged in arresting and taking Jews to the concentration camp, where after one day they were given 'special handling' (*Sonderbehandlung*).

The integration of the Lithuanians into E.K.9 activity made it possible to increase the number of Jews kidnapped and killed daily at Ponar. The E.K.9 was organized in such a way that each stage and type of *Aktion* had its own special force, permitting the operation to be carried out simultaneously.

Diary of the Vilna Ghetto

Herman Kruk, director of the Grosser Library in Warsaw, escaped in the second week of the German attack on that city and reached Vilna after several weeks. He resolved to cast his lot with the Vilna Jewry and remained in that city. He also decided to chronicle the events of those turbulent times.

The diary begins with the panic that seized Vilna on hearing the news of the German military attack on Russia, in June 1941. It runs for 603 pages before ending abruptly on 14 July 1943. Its author was taken to Estonia, where he died in September 1944 aged 47.

What follows are extracts translated from the Yiddish of the diary, reprinted by permission of the YIVO Institute for Jewish Research, New York.

Saturday, September 6, [1941]
The Historic Day – Entry into the Ghetto
Six thirty in the morning. It could have been expected that the order to transfer to the Ghetto would be received as a dreadful decree of confinement, as tidings of horror, but it had not been so. Vilna has received the order calmly and with discipline.

They came early this morning and allowed half an hour for packing. Thereby sadism attained to a high degree of refinement.

Nine o'clock. Groups of Jews are being led. They drag and haul things in baby carriages. People have rigged up boards and carry things on them. Wheelbarrows are pushed. A heart-rending picture.

Two o'clock in the afternoon. We eat our lunch (perhaps the last) seated on our bundles. The landlady urges on: eat up everything. Leave nothing . . .

January 20 [1942]
The Writers and Artists Association
This Sunday there was organized in the Ghetto an association of writers and artists.

April 24 [1942]

No Insane

This is highly characteristic for our time and life. A normal community of about twenty thousand people would have a considerable number of people who go insane. Here in the Ghetto, where everything is abnormal and unusual, there are hardly any cases of insanity.

April 27 [1942]

Opening of the Ghetto Theatre

Last night the premiere of the Ghetto Theatre at the Culture Department took place in the hall of the former so-called Little Municipal Hall.

May 3 [1942]

Hunger Knocks on the Door

One of the employees in our office asked me to assign him to a job at which he could sit, for he cannot stand up. Dr Feinstein complained that he had not eaten for three days. If he could only get some carrots.

July 25 [1942]

Ponar as He Saw It

And here I am in possession of an authentic report on Ponar – from a Jew who was there, wandering among the mass graves.

The area is covered with a thin forest and cut by large trenches and pits. The pits have a diameter of 30–40 metres and a depth of about 6 metres. Some are smaller. Around every pit there is a wall of dug-out earth. Some of the pits are half filled-in, others completely. Their contents are indicated by the pungent odour.

Here and there parts of human bodies protrude from the ground; often entire bodies. Scattered about are documents, purses, small mirrors, torn paper money, cartridges, machine-gun and automatic-rifle bullets.

September 29 [1942]

Theatre in the Ghetto

The theatre resumed activity with renewed vigour. If September was devoted mainly to repeating the old favourites, October should be a month of premieres, new pieces that may possibly win the plaudits of the theatregoers.

In preparation is a revue titled 'You Never Can Tell', which, patently, has relevance to our precarious times.

December 14 [1942]
Ghetto Industry
As indicated previously, we are constantly moving in the direction of establishing a great industrial centre in the Ghetto. To be sure, it is not so much we as it is the Germans who are pushing us in that direction. They want Jewish productivity to become a source of exploitation for their military purposes.

December 18 [1942]
Three Minutes of Silence
Only now the world has discovered that the Germans are killing Jews by the hundreds of thousands. Only now!

We have frequently recorded the campaign on that front. Today I have learned on the radio that the governments of London, the U.S.S.R and the United States of America have issued today a joint declaration on the persecution of Jews in all countries occupied by the Germans.

March 3 [1943]
A Complete School System
At the opening of the Girls Boarding School one of the teachers stated that we have nowadays in the Ghetto a complete school system. I believe he is right.

March 25 [1943]
The Picture Is Becoming Clearer
The Gestapo is now forwarding reports that the number of Jews in the Ghetto has risen to 23 or 24 thousand. It recommends a reduction to 15 or 16 thousand. This means that some six or eight thousand people will have to be taken out of the Ghetto.

Tomorrow the Premiere of Pinski's 'Treasure'
Meanwhile all goes on as before. After long preparations tomorrow evening Pinski's 'Treasure' will be presented at the Ghetto theatre. I am reliably informed that all tickets for tomorrow's performance as well as the following three evenings have been sold out.

April 5 [1943]
Over 4,000 in 83 Railway Cars
Now it is clear: instead of going to Kaunas, the trains from Osmiany and Swienciany went to Ponar . . . The 83 cars carried over 4,000 Jewish victims.

April 12 [1943]

What do the Escapees Tell?

On Sunday, April 4, the Jews of Swienciany were loaded on railway cars. At 10 o'clock in the morning the train – doors locked and windows barred with barbed wire – departed. None of the passengers had the slightest misgivings. 'We had the full assurance of the Jewish police,' the narrator added ironically.

About 11 o'clock on Sunday evening the train arrived in Vilna. The passengers slept in the cars. Monday morning at 10 o'clock the train departed from Vilna and within about an hour arrived in Ponar. Immediately the train was surrounded by German and Lithuanian soldiers. A gruesome panic ensued. The cries and laments virtually pierced the heavens.

Shortly several cars were opened and a fusillade was heard. The narrator's car was fourth and was opened about 1 o'clock noon. Up to that time the Jews saw through the windows how the people were driven from the cars, how some attempted to escape, how they were shot at . . . The narrator's car contained 52 people. They were taken out and led in the direction of the wire fence. Some 20 metres before the fence the narrator decided to run away. Practically all in the group followed suit. This was their salvation, for the Germans and Lithuanians could not shoot simultaneously at all of them. Thus several escaped. Two of this group have arrived in the Ghetto. The others, the narrator hopes, will still come.

May 16 [1943]

The Ghetto Industry

The number of students in the technical schools has gone up to 100. The second tailoring shop is moving to Rudnicka Street 13. It will take on 50 additional workers. Huge military orders have been received.

June 12 [1943]

A Hebrew Performance

Two days ago the premiere of the Hebrew Dramatic Studio took place. The play was David Pinski's 'Eternal Jew,' and the players mostly policemen.

June 22 [? 1943]

A Powder Keg

The Ghetto is beginning to resemble a powder keg, which may explode any minute.

July 2 [1943]

'The Forest' – a Mass Phenomenon

Escape to the forest has lately become virtually a mass phenomenon. As soon as some kind of a raid occurs the Christians take to the forest. Jewish young men go to the forest, as well as Poles, Lithuanians, White Russians, Ukrainians.

July 4 [1943]

New Military Orders

The Ghetto shops are expanding in response to the increased military orders for goods. The latest orders are for one hundred thousand pairs of socks and twenty thousand pairs of boots.

July 14 [1943]

To Be on Guard!

The condemned are entitled to know the time of the execution of their sentence. Don't we know for certain that our fate is sealed?

And the Ghetto Industry Is Expanding

What is happening here is not only amazing but truly insensate. Here we stand awaiting the angel of death and at the same time we stand in the 'alien' shop, whetting the knife aimed at our throat. While we wait for the slaughterer, we are expanding our Ghetto Industry . . .

The Vilna Ghetto Theatre

[Extracts from 'The Cultural Life of the Vilna Ghetto' by Solon Beinfeld, from the *Simon Wiesenthal Center Annual, Volume One*.]

Vilna, the Lithuanian Jerusalem, was for centuries one of the great centres of Jewish creativity. Nearly all the great modern Jewish movements in culture and politics . . . are closely associated with Vilna, a city where tradition and modernization harmoniously mingled.

In its last years, as a ghetto under Nazi rule, this ancient community did not betray its cultural heritage. As Isaiah Trunk writes in his book *Judenrat*, confronted with 'the uncommonly rich documentation of cultural activities in the Vilna Ghetto, one is often tempted not to believe that such colourful, almost "normal" cultural work took place in a ghetto where remnants of a decimated community were concentrated, constantly in danger of destruction.'

But this 'normalcy' is of course an illusion, and was understood to be an illusion, perhaps even a dangerous one, at the time. The Vilna Ghetto was in fact ambivalent towards its own cultural activity, and the reasons for this need to be discussed along with the astonishing cultural achievements themselves. This ambivalence is perhaps most clearly evident in connection with the Ghetto Theatre, in some respects the most striking form of cultural activity in the ghetto. At the Nuremberg Trials, on 10 August 1946, Israel Segal testified that 'I was director of the ghetto theatre which the Germans forced us to keep going.' Segal's statement is false: the Germans were quite indifferent to this aspect of the internal life of the ghetto. But it is nevertheless revealing for the sense of disbelief and shame which, after the war, became attached to the very notion of theatre in the ghetto because of the suspicion that in some way it might ultimately have served the Germans' purposes. The same year, in an article for a Yiddish-language journal, Segal was more candid. He placed the responsibility for the beginnings of theatrical activity on Jacob Gens, the head of Jewish police and 'dictator' of the Vilna Ghetto. But Segal's true feelings are perhaps best revealed in a

speech he gave in July 1942, at a 'coffee' sponsored by the
Theatre Section of the Cultural Department of the Vilna ghetto
administration on the occasion of the six-month anniversary of
the Ghetto Theatre. Six months was a long time in the
compressed chronology of the ghetto, and Segal reminisced about
the remote time when Gens had first proposed a concert. This
proposal was 'not only a daring step, it was a daring beginning to
the forced normalization of ghetto life'. The concert had taken
place 'despite the great protests of various influential persons and
community activists'. It had been hard to convince even fellow-
actors that 'theatre may indeed be performed in a cemetery'.

This last was a reference to the bitter slogan, *'oyf a beysoylom
shpilt men nit kayn teater'* ('in a cemetery no theatre is to be
performed'), which had been posted all over the ghetto by the
Socialist *Bund* in response to the announcement of the first
concert. This reflected the widespread indignation in the ghetto
and at the same time constituted the first open defiance of the
Gens regime.

However, nobody seems to have quarrelled with the
programme of the concert itself, which took place on Sunday
evening, 18 January 1942 (four months after the establishment of
the ghetto, and two months after the deportation of half its
inhabitants), in the hall of the former Yiddish *gymnasium* where
the Judenrat now had its offices. The audience was largely
composed of ghetto-policeman and ghetto-notables with their
families, but all factions sent observers to see whether the honour
and mourning of the ghetto would be desecrated. By all accounts
the concert was on a high level, in no way insulting to the feelings
of the community. The programme consisted among other things
of poetry by classic Jewish authors such as Bialik and Peretz, a
dramatization of a short story by Stefan Zweig, a Chopin
Nocturne and a new work by the young ghetto poet Sutskever.
Gens' second-in-command, the highly regarded Joseph Glazman
(later one of the leaders of the resistance), opened the concert
with a semi-apology and a memorial prayer for the dead.

The effect of this dignified performance, in the best Vilna
tradition, was enormous. To some – as Gens had intended – it
meant nothing less than a turning point in the history of the
Ghetto. Dr Lazar Epstein mentions in his diary that he had feared
the evening would be a scandal, that the Germans would
photograph it and use it in their propaganda. Instead, 'people
laughed and cried. They cast off the depression that had been
weighing on their spirits. The alienation that had hitherto existed

among the ghetto-population seemed to have been thrown off . . .
People awoke from a long, difficult dream.'

Thereafter, opposition to the theatre faded. Performances were
frequent and well-attended, and a major source of revenue for
ghetto charities. As an institution, the theatre remained
particularly dear to Gens, who never forgave the *Bund* for its
handbills. For Gens, the theatre was always more than a cultural
ornament or a source of employment for actors, musicians and
artists (though he was quite sensitive to this need). It remained
throughout the existence of the ghetto, a principal instrument of
'forced normalization' and an important calming influence on a
ghetto population living in constant fear and uncertainty. In a
report of the Cultural Department for November 1942 this point
is explicitly made:

> In mid-November there spread through the ghetto
> unfounded rumours, which might have provoked panic. The
> Ghetto Theatre received an order (from Gens) to organize
> two popular performances in order to calm the public. Such
> performances took place the 18th and 19th November . . .
> The tickets to both performances were proof of the
> popularity of the Ghetto Theatre and of its great calming
> effect on the public.

By the time of the second concert, which took place one week
after the first (25 January 1942), inhibitions concerning the theatre
had so far receded that the presence of invited German and
Lithuanian dignitaries, among them well-known murderers of
Vilna Jewry, excited no public protest, whatever the private
feelings of the audience.

The hall of the former *gymnasium* on Rudnicka Street 6 was
evidently inadequate, so plans were pushed for remodelling the
former small municipal auditorium on Konska Street, whose
entrance was outside the ghetto, but which backed on to the
Judenrat complex on Rudnicka Street. Although small concerts
(under the patronage of the ghetto police) continued for a time to
be given in the old hall, the real opening of the theatre 'season'
came on Sunday evening 26 April 1942, this time under the
sponsorship of the Cultural Department. The diarist Kruk, a
Bundist and bitter opponent of the Gens regime, managed to find
a few good words for this inaugural event.

The seating was significant, and changed with the political
vicissitudes of various ghetto personalities. A 'Chart of Reserved
Seats of Invitees to Premieres – 1943 Vilna Ghetto' gives a rough

idea of the power structure following the Gens *coup d'état* of July 1942 which ended nominal supremacy of the Judenrat. Two seats for Dessler (the police chief), Fryd (former chairman of the Judenrat, now head of the ghetto-administration), and their wives. Further to the sides and in the second row are seats for heads of administrative departments and higher police officers, and influential persons like Kaplan-Kaplanski, Chairman of the Council of Brigadiers (i.e. leaders of labour units working for the Germans outside the ghetto, on whom Gens depended heavily for the success of his 'rescue-through-work' strategy). Further back, in the third through fifth rows appear cultural leaders like Kruk (head of the ghetto-library), the directors of the Hebrew and Yiddish choruses and the poet Sutskever. For Gens, the Ghetto Theatre had become the Versailles of his tiny kingdom.

In April 1942 the theatre gave one performance, with 315 in the audience. By November, there were 19 performances and 5,846 patrons that month. The total to 10 January 1943 was 111 performances, with 34,804 tickets sold. Most theatricals continued to be of the revue variety, mixing songs, instrumental numbers and dramatic sketches. The revenue *Korene Yorn un Vey Tsu di Teg* ('Years of Rye and Woe to the Days') featured songs by Sasriel Broydo the 'folk poet' of the ghetto, whose simple, topical themes became immensely popular. In *Korene Yorn*, which opened in July 1942, Broydo's hit song was 'Efsher Vet Geshen a Nes' ('Perhaps a Miracle Will Occur') with the refrain:

> Perhaps a miracle will occur
> Perhaps a miracle will occur
> True, it's hard to say
> It's hard to bear the burden
> But perhaps a miracle will occur.

The revue sequence continued in October 1942 with the opening of *Men Kon Gornit Visn* (You Never Can Tell). The title refers, as Kruk explains it, to the rumour-filled atmosphere of the ghetto, where the comment, 'you never can tell', instantly 'makes you a certified wise man in the eyes of young and old'. The principal author again was Broydo. The semi-official ghetto (mimeographed) newspaper *Geto Yedies* (*News of the Ghetto*) reviewed the production on 11 October 1942:

> 'You Never Can Tell'
>
> This secretive – playful, intriguing saying is the Leitmotiv of the new revue at the Ghetto Theatre. It has already played

four times, each time to a packed house. The revue pleases, amuses. Most numbers grow out of our ghetto-reality, show pictures of our life with good-natured humour, often sarcastically exaggerated. A novelty is the number 'Melokhe-Melukhe' ('Craft-State'), which seeks to popularize the idea of productive labour. As a first try, it succeeded fairly well. But . . . if such productions are to achieve their aim, they must not be boring. The white net of propaganda must be invisible.

The next revue, *Peshe Fun Reshe* (*Peshe from Rzesza*) opened in June 1943, at a time when the labour camps in the Vilna region, including Rzesza, were being liquidated, and some of their inmates brought to the Vilna Ghetto. Leyb Rozenthal's song for the revue, 'Baym Geto-toyer' ('By the Ghetto-Gate') also known as 'Tsu eyns tsvey dray' ('One, two, three') describing the selections at the time of the great deportations of the autumn of 1941, quickly became a folksong, still heard today.

The last of the revues, *Moyshe Halt Zikh* (*Moshe Hold On*), opened amidst the deportations to Estonia which marked the last phase of the ghetto (August–September 1943); it was not uncommon for the deportees leaving for Estonia in the morning to go to the theatre for the last time the previous evening. The title song, by Broydo, was a call to endurance:

> Moyshe, hold on
> Hold on Moyshe
> It is not far off
> Soon the great hour will strike.

The revues, for all their timeliness and popularity, give only a partial picture of theatre in the ghetto. There was a little theatre, playing in the cafe on Rudnicka Street 13, called *Di Yogenish in Fas* (*The Rush into the Barrel*, a pun on Diogenes). There were numerous symphonic and choral concerts (the Yiddish and Hebrew choruses were both very active), children's performances of various kinds, a huge number of literary evenings, workers' lectures, popular medical talks, etc., all of which belong to ghetto cultural life in the broader sense rather than to theatre properly speaking. But above all else there was the impressive series of five full-scale dramas (four in Yiddish, one in Hebrew), that are by any standard the highpoint of the cultural achievements of the ghetto and in every way worthy of the best traditions of Jewish theatre in Eastern Europe.

The first of these, *Grine Felder* (*Green Fields*), a well-known pastoral romance by the Yiddish-American playwright Peretz Hirschbein, chosen in part to bring a bit of nature into a ghetto where there was exactly one tree, opened in August 1942, and played some 28 times to packed houses. In late November 1942 came the premiere of *Der Mentsch Untern Brik* (*The Man Under the Bridge*), a translation (with Jewish names for the characters) of a play by the Hungarian dramatist Otto Indig. The play deals with an unemployed doctor who turns to crime, contemplates suicide and is finally rehabilitated. This might seem an odd choice for the ghetto (though its upbeat moral was relevant enough), but it must be remembered that the pre-war Yiddish theatre in Vilna had been very cosmopolitan and the report of the Cultural Department for November 1942 describes the opening with great pride as 'a normal European premiere, which would have been a success in Vilna even before the war'. At the end of March 1943, came the premiere of David Pinski's well-known comedy *Der Oytser* (*The Treasure*). In his diary, Herman Kruk noted the contrast between this festive occasion and the brutal reality outside, in this case the liquidation of the provincial ghettos:

> Saturday the 27th (of March), in a hall filled to capacity, there took place the premiere of *Oytser*. Outside, the police were guarding the arrivals from Swieciany, here in the theatre, as if nothing were happening – a premiere! The performance is smooth, the play is unblemished, the sets really beautiful – as if this were not the Ghetto.

The sole Hebrew-language theatrical production in the Ghetto (apart from a Chanukah pageant put on by the boys of *Yeladim*, the transport-brigade organized for homeless and delinquent children) was also by Pinski. His *Ha-yehudi Ha-nitskhi* (*The Eternal Jew*) opened on 10 June 1943, under the sponsorship of the Hebrew Drama Studio, a branch of the *Brit Ivrit* (*Hebrew Union*) which in addition supported the Hebrew Chorus and a number of other Hebrew-language cultural activities. In its choice of this play, set in the period of the Jewish revolt against Rome and the destruction of the Second Temple, the youthful and dynamic Zionist segment of the Ghetto was freer to touch on the great Ghetto theme of revolt and armed struggle than was the case with the Yiddish theatre, which had had to cancel a planned production of *Bar Kochba* for fear of the Germans. For the Zionists, this was a triumphant collective achievement, with various Hebraists assisting in the reconstruction of the text, and biblical costumes for the crowd scenes fashioned from prayer shawls.

The last theatrical production, *Der Mabl* (*The Flood*), a translation of *Syndafloden* by the Swedish dramatist Henning Berger, opened during the summer of 1943, in the last weeks of the Ghetto's existence. This story of the trials of a group of people trapped in an American saloon during a flood might again seem an odd choice for the Vilna Ghetto, but the moral – that people pull together during times of common danger, but revert to petty divisions when the danger appears to fade – was relevant enough.

Despite the ominous signs of the approaching liquidation of the Ghetto, plans for the coming theatre season went forward, with Sholom Aleichem's *Tevye der Milkhiker* (*Tevye the Milkman*) [the play on which *Fiddler on the Roof* was later based] as the next production. It had not yet opened when the end came in September 1943.

GHETTO

Characters

SRULIK (the NARRATOR), a ventriloquist and actor, aged 30
the DUMMY
KITTEL, a Nazi officer (also plays DR PAUL)
WEISKOPF, an entrepreneur, in his forties
HAYYAH, a singer, in her twenties
GENS, head of the ghetto, in his forties
the HASSID, in his thirties
KRUK, the ghetto librarian, in his forties
JUDITH, an actress (plays WEINER, a young physician)
OOMA, an actress
GOTTLIEB, an elderly physician
a JUDGE, aged forty-five
a RABBI, aged fifty
LUBA,
YANKEL,
GEIVISH, } young black-marketeers
ELIA
DESSLER, Jewish ghetto police officer, aged thirty-five
ACTORS, DANCERS, MUSICIANS
HAIKIN, a musician

Note

Ghetto is one of three related plays by Joshua Sobol set in the
Vilna ghetto. The other two in the triptych are *Adam*, about the
resistance movement, and *Underground*, dealing with the dilemmas
facing the medical staff in the ghetto hospital. Neither has yet
been staged in English.

The lyrics and melody lines for the songs in *Ghetto* are at the end
of the book and their order of performance for the National
Theatre production was correct at the time of going to press,
although rehearsals were not completed. The songs can, however,
be sung in different sequence for different productions.

Erratum

During rehearsal certain names of characters in the Vilna Theatre
Company were changed.   The full list is now as follows:

The Theatre Company

YOSEF GERSTEIN	the Hassid and the Rabbi	David Schneider
JUDITH AZRA	the woman	Nicola Scott
OOMAH ORSHEVSKAYA	Dr Weiner	Angela Pleasence
YITSHOK ELMIS	Dr Gottlieb	Jon Rumney
AVROM BLIAKHER	the Judge	Nicholas Blane
LUBA GRODZENSKI		Laura Shavin
ELIA GEIVISH	black-marketeers	Mark Lockyer
YITZHOK GEIVISH		Glyn Pritchard
YANKEL POLIKANSKI		Mark Addy
ALEXANDER GERTNER	trumpeter	Jo Stone-Fewings
SHABSE GOTTLIB	bass player	Sandy Burnett
SONIA GRUDBERG		Sandra Butterworth
HAIKIN	violinist	Vladimir Asrlev
YAKOB IRIS		Ged McKenna
HELENA LARES		Jill Stanford
YITZHOK LIPOVSK		John Fitzgerald Jay
SHMUEL MANDELBLIT	trumpeter	Oliver Beamish
SASHA MOLEVSKY		Ivan Kaye
NEMI NADIR	violinist	Judith Sim
BARUCH NATAN		Trevor Sellers
YAKOB NEMI	guitarist	Michael O'Connor
MOISHE NORVID	saxophonist	Merlin Shepherd
LEAH RUDKOV		Jennifer Hill
ZIGMUND SAMBERG	clarinettist	David Roach
AVROM WITTENBERG		Tam Dean Burn
HENRY TAYTLBOYM	trombonist	Keith Woodhams
AVROM VALTER	accordionist	Brian Greene
POLIA WITTENBERG		Sandy McDade
		Christopher Armstrong
		Melvyn Bedford
GESTAPO GUARDS		Toby E. Byrne
		Ciaran McIntyre
JEWISH POLICE		Mark Addy
OFFICERS		Christopher Armstrong
		Melvyn Bedford
		John Fitzgerald Jay
		Mark Lockyer
		Glyn Pritchard
		Trevor Sellers

Ghetto was first staged in Great Britain in the Olivier auditorium of the National Theatre.

First preview was 20 April 1989; press night was 27 April 1989.

The cast was as follows:

SRULIK	*ventriloquist and director*	Jonathan Cullen
KITTEL also DR PAUL	*SS Officer*	Alex Jennings
HAYYAH	*singer*	Maria Friedman
DJIGAN	*the Dummy*	Linda Kerr Scott
GENS	*Chief of Jewish Police*	John Woodvine
WEISKOPF	*tailor*	Anthony O'Donnell
KRUK	*Ghetto Librarian*	Paul Jesson
DESSLER	*Jewish police officer*	Ivan Kaye

The Theatre Company:

YOSEF GERSTEIN	*the Hassid and the Rabbi*	David Schneider
JUDITH LARES	*the woman*	Nicola Scott
OOMA ORSHEVESKAYA	*Dr Weiner*	Angela Pleasance
YITSHOK SAMBER	*Dr Gottlieb*	Jon Rumney
AVROM MOLEVSKY	*the Judge*	Nicholas Blane
LUBA GRODZINSKI		Laura Shavin
ELIA GEIVISH		Mark Lockyer
YITZHOK GEIVISH	*black marketeers*	Glyn Pritchard
YANKEL POLIKANSKI		Mark Addy
ALEXANDER AZRA	*trumpeter*	Jo Stone-Fewings
SHABSE BLIAKHER	*bass player and violinist*	Sandy Burnett
SONIA ELMIS		Sandra Butterworth

YAKOB GERTNER		Ged McKenna
HELENA GOTTLIB		Jill Stanford
YITZHOK GRUDBERG		John Fitzgerald Jay
HAIKIN	*violinist*	Vladimir Asriev
SHMUEL IRIS	*trumpeter*	Oliver Beamish
SASHA LIPOVSK		Ivan Kaye
YAKOB MANDELBLIT	*guitarist*	Michael O'Connor
BARUCH NADIR		Trevor Sellers
NEMI NATAN	*violinist*	Judith Sim
LEAH NEMI		Jennifer Hill
MOISHE NORVID	*saxophonist*	Merlin Shepherd
ZIGMUND RUDKOV	*clarinettist*	David Roach
HENRY TARLO	*trombonist*	Keith Woodhams
AVROM TAYTLBOYM	*accordionist*	Brian Greene
POLIA VALTER		Sandy McDade
AVROM WITTENBERG		Tam Dean Burn

GESTAPO GUARDS:
{ Christopher Armstrong
Melvyn Bedford
Toby E Byrne
Ciaran McIntyre

JEWISH POLICE OFFICERS
{ Mark Addy
Christopher Armstrong
Melvyn Bedford
John Fitzgerald Jay
Mark Lockyer
Glyn Pritchard
Trevor Sellers

Directed by   Nicholas Hytner
Designed by   Bob Crowley

PART ONE

Scene One

1983. The living room of a middle-class apartment in Tel Aviv. Very clean and tidy. In an armchair sits the NARRATOR, *an old man wearing a bathrobe. He has only one hand. The* NARRATOR *is being interviewed by an unseen person.*

NARRATOR. Our last performance? I remember nothing.

Our last performance . . . It was the night before Kittel murdered Gens. Ten days later the ghetto was destroyed. That was the last performance.

A good house? Listen to what I'm going to tell you. The theatre was full. Not even standing room. Every time we put on a show, sold out three weeks in advance! Never mind the misery, the fear – that's how it was. People who knew next day they'd be on a train to the camps, the night before they'd put on their finery, came to the play.

Yes, yes, the last one, I'm right. By then Gens was head of the ghetto. When the Gestapo came for him I was sitting in his office reading plays. I was artistic director. I had to decide, what shall we do next? We had a competition: write a play about life in the ghetto. Entries poured in. Katrielka Broide, Leibeleh Rosental, Hirschke Glick, Israel Diamantman . . . Everyone wrote one. Marvellous plays. Full of life! All of them lost. Real works of art! Gone. What remains?

I remember . . . a scene here, a scene there.

Well, we *wanted* to stage the winning entry but ten days later . . .

Somewhere I've got a few songs from the cabaret, our small auditorium. We put on satirical reviews. '*Die Yoganesh in Fass*'. Do you get it? It's a pun. Diogenes, you know, the philosopher, he lived in a barrel. Diogenes – *die yoganesh*, which means running around. In a barrel – *in fass*. 'Running around in a barrel.' And we were! He was looking for justice. We were looking for justice. Could we find it?

Can I find it? *'Die Yoganesh'*. Maybe in my library. I don't remember . . .

He stands. Moving is an effort for him. Suddenly he bounds forward and passes through the wall. The walls of the apartment vanish. The stage is empty all the way to the wings.

Scene Two

Darkness. An iron gate. To one side, piles of metal chairs. The clinking of locks, the rattling of chains, the squeaking of bolts. The gate opens wide with a thud. A truck reverses in. It brakes sharply and stops. The back section tips up depositing a huge pile of clothes onto the stage. The motor is turned off. Through the gates, the sound of a raging storm and fierce winds. The shadow of KITTEL, *a German officer, appears at the gate. He wears a long army coat, boots and a helmet. He carries a gun (a Schmeisser) in one hand, a long black case in the other. With a torch* KITTEL *lights up the back of the truck revealing the huge pile of clothes.*

KITTEL. Chaos!

WEISKOPF, *his clothing tattered and caked with mud, stands near* KITTEL *who shines his torch on the fuse box. To* WEISKOPF:

Let there be light!

WEISKOPF *throws a switch. Industrial lamps cast a dim glow over the stage.*

More light!

WEISKOPF *turns on more lights. A group of shadows appears and approaches. They are women and men, emotionally and physically exhausted. They wear filthy rags. The* NARRATOR, SRULIK, *is standing near this group. He now has both hands.*

SRULIK. I remember . . . we had to keep walking and walking. We came to a huge pile of clothes.

KITTEL. Some are dry, some are soaking. Some are men's, some are women's, some are children's. Sort them. Begin!

The group divides into two. Some bring clothes forward and sort them into separate piles. Others bring clothes from the truck, then go backwards and forwards bringing ever more clothes to be sorted. Despite their exhaustion, they work efficiently, mechanically. KITTEL watches with indifference. From a dark corner HAYYAH appears. Wrapped in a ragged blanket, she shivers from the cold. Her hair is dishevelled, her bare feet filthy from wading through mud. She stops a short way from KITTEL and watches the back and forth movement of those carrying clothes. KITTEL sees HAYYAH, shines his torch on her.

HAYYAH. Please . . . a pair of shoes?

KITTEL. Over here.

HAYYAH walks towards him, stops a short distance away.

KITTEL. You wanted?

HAYYAH. A pair of shoes.

KITTEL. Don't you realise whose shoes they were? (*He watches her.*) Well, now you do. So help yourself, any pair you fancy.

HAYYAH hesitates, then goes to the pile, sits, tries on shoes. KITTEL shines his torch on her from a distance. Some of the workers watch anxiously, others go on with their work. HAYYAH finds a pair of boots that fit, gets up, hurries away, reaches the wings.

KITTEL. Over here!

HAYYAH goes to him. KITTEL indicates the cloak of rags she wears.

Off.

HAYYAH takes it off, revealing a torn slip.

So many dresses and no-one to wear them. Choose.

HAYYAH shakes her head.

Do it!

HAYYAH goes to the pile of women's clothes, selects a dress.

Put it on.

She does.

Now a coat.

She puts one on.

Why not a hat?

She takes a beret from a pile of hats.

Over here.

She goes closer to him.

I said, here!

He shines the torch in her face.

Hold your chin up. Smooth your hair. Now, the beret.

She puts it on.

Delicious. When you Jews are beautiful, you're the most
beautiful of all. Turn.

She turns. He notices a swelling over her stomach.

What's that?

He jabs the butt of his Schmeisser into her stomach.

You know you're not allowed to get pregnant. Didn't you think
what they'll do to you? Lost your tongue? Over here!

She goes even closer. He feels her stomach, laughs.

Take it out.

HAYYAH *takes a paper bag from under her slip.* KITTEL *holds out his
hand and she gives it to him. He turns it over. Beans scatter everywhere.*
KITTEL *reads the label.*

'Beans. One kilo.' The black market. From whom did you buy
it? I want names.

She says nothing.

You didn't buy it. It's stolen. You stole a kilo of beans from the
army store. Turn! To the wall, march!

HAYYAH *walks towards the wall, stops.* KITTEL *cocks the Schmeisser,
takes aim.* SRULIK *has been holding an armful of clothes and watching.
Now he drops them and rushes towards* KITTEL. *With him is a*
DUMMY. SRULIK *ventriloquises the* DUMMY's *voice in such a way
that it seems to be the* DUMMY *who takes the lead and* SRULIK *who
holds him back.*

DUMMY. Wait! *Halt! Arretez! Stoi!*

SRULIK (*to the* DUMMY). Don't do that! You're a hero, it's me
who gets shot in the head.

DUMMY. Who cares about your head?

SRULIK. I do. I'm attached to it.

DUMMY. It's Hayyah! Aren't you a man? Defend her.

SRULIK. A man? No, just a Jew. I surrender.

DUMMY. Just a Jew? And you're proud of it?

SRULIK. I'll hang my head but I'll hang onto it.

KITTEL (*to* SRULIK *and the* DUMMY). Over here!

They go to him.

Who are you?

DUMMY (*pointing at* SRULIK). That's who gave her the beans!

KITTEL (*to* SRULIK). Is it true?

SRULIK. He's lying.

DUMMY. *I'm* lying?

SRULIK. He'll say anything to finish me off.

DUMMY. He'll say anything to stay alive! (*To* KITTEL:) Blow out his brains! Free the world from this rat!

KITTEL. Enough.

SRULIK (*to the* DUMMY). See?

DUMMY. You heard him?

SRULIK. He's talking to you.

DUMMY. Me?

SRULIK. You heard him.

DUMMY. He's talking to you!

KITTEL (*to the* DUMMY). Shut up! Or I'll shoot out your throat. (*To* SRULIK:) Did you give her the beans?

Silence.

SRULIK. If I had beans, I'd eat them myself. She wouldn't dirty her hands in the black market. She's a singer.

DUMMY (*to* KITTEL). You see? He's absurd. She croons – la la la.

SRULIK. She's a remarkable artist.

DUMMY. He's cracked about her.

SRULIK. Before the war she was a star. These days . . . When was her last engagement? She's starving! That's why I appeal to you. After all, you're an artist, she's an artist . . .

DUMMY. Don't flatter him. Kittel hates arselickers.

KITTEL *laughs.*

KITTEL. You understand me.

DUMMY (*to* SRULIK). You see? Art has nothing to do with it. What if she had lost her voice? Would she have no right to live?

KITTEL, *very amused, laughs loudly. Then, suddenly serious:*

KITTEL. Everyone, over here!

Everyone stops what they're doing and moves towards KITTEL.

You! Bring those scales.

Someone fetches the scales. KITTEL *puts the bean bag on them.*

In one minute every bean will be back in the bag. Begin!

Everyone scurries frantically round gathering beans, putting them in the bag. KITTEL *looks at his watch.*

Stop!

He looks at the scales:

Nine hundred and forty grams. And the other sixty? How will you repay your debt?

He hums a few bars of a song to himself. Then to HAYYAH:

Shall I use this? (*Pointing to the Schmeisser.*) Or that? (*Pointing to a long black case.*)

HAYYAH *hesitates a long time.*

HAYYAH (*of the case*). That.

KITTEL *chuckles, kneels, opens the case slowly, takes out an object wrapped in rags. Gradually he peels off the covering and reveals a saxophone. He plays a few notes of a German song, 'There once was a king in Tulla'.*

KITTEL. Do you know it?

HAYYAH *nods.*

Then sing!

KITTEL *plays.* HAYYAH *opens her mouth but no sound comes out. He stops.*

That Jew said you're a singer. Was he lying? You'll both be in Ponar by morning. You won't want to sing there. Sing!

HAYYAH *opens her mouth, tries to sing, can't. Pointing to her throat:*

HAYYAH. Dry.

KITTEL. Why didn't you say so?

He takes out a hip flask, hands it to her. She drinks, hands it back.

HAYYAH. Please, one of our songs.

KITTEL. *S'il vous plaît, Madame! S'il vous plaît!*

HAYYAH *sings.*

SONG NUMBER ONE.

KITTEL. You sing well, Jewess. I'm very moved. Look. (*He shows them a tear he has wept.*) That was worth ten grams. Fifty to go. How will you make them up to me?

Silence.

You're all artists, right?

DUMMY. We are! The whole lot of us!

KITTEL. This will be your theatre. I'll order the ghetto council. I'm giving you a chance to prove art is worth fifty grams of beans. But I warn you, I'm a connoisseur. You can't palm off rubbish on me.

He goes. Everyone leaves, except HAYYAH, SRULIK, *the* DUMMY *and an* ACTOR *who searches obsessively through the pile of clothes.*

HAYYAH (*to* SRULIK). I can't ever thank you.

DUMMY. Of course you can. Easy.

SRULIK. You owe nothing.

DUMMY. What's stopping you? Say what you feel!

SRULIK. I'm glad you're alive, that's the end of it.

HAYYAH. He could have killed you!

SRULIK. If he did? What's my life?

DUMMY. 'Without you.' Say it! 'What's my life without you?'

SRULIK. I'm nothing. A ventriloquist. A bit-part player.

HAYYAH. A hero. (*She kisses him.*)

DUMMY. No, no! I saved you! He tried to stop me! Hayyah'leh, sweetheart, you owe your life to me!

HAYYAH. You're sweet. (*She pats the* DUMMY's *head.*)

DUMMY. Ohhh! Oooh! Aaah! It's been so long. Now my turn.

The DUMMY *feels her up.*

SRULIK. Stop it. You should be ashamed!

DUMMY. He's jealous! (*To* SRULIK.) Park yourself over there – further, further – good. (*To* HAYYAH:) You do love me, don't you?

HAYYAH (*laughing*). It's impossible not to.

DUMMY. I adore you. From the moment I laid – eyes on you. Hayyah'leh, little one, skinny little . . . You're starving! (*To* SRULIK:) Give her something to eat!

SRULIK. I've got nothing.

DUMMY. Liar! Turn out your pockets!

SRULIK *turns out one pocket. It's empty.*

Other one! Other one!

SRULIK *turns out the other pocket and finds a carrot.*

SRULIK. I forgot.

DUMMY. And you want her to want you?

SRULIK. Take it. (*He hands her the carrot.*)

HAYYAH. But you . . .

DUMMY. Ha! You wouldn't have got that if he didn't have another.

SRULIK *pulls out another carrot.*

See? Enjoy.

SRULIK *and* HAYYAH *eat.*

You're enjoying? So, where do you sleep?

HAYYAH. Me? In the stairwell.

DUMMY. Why not sleep with us?

SRULIK. What's got into you?

DUMMY. We've got plenty of room.

SRULIK. To even suggest it!

DUMMY. Do you keep me warm? (*To* HAYYAH:) I want to be warm. Is that a sin?

HAYYAH. No, my little one. I'm so sick of cold nights. I also want to be warm. Come on, let's go.

DUMMY (*to* SRULIK). Put your arm round her, idiot.

(SRULIK *does.*)

Tighter! Must I tell you everything?

SONG NUMBER TWO.

HAYYAH *and the* DUMMY *go.* SRULIK *remains. He looks around.*

Scene Three

GENS *enters, walks over to* SRULIK.

GENS. Srulik! What do you know! There is a God in heaven. How long have I wanted to give you a theatre? Everywhere opposition. Today the council orders me: do it! So, what do you think? Is this place suitable?

SRULIK. In what sense?

GENS. Are there enough seats? Count them.

SRULIK. It's the first thing I did.

GENS. And the stage?

SRULIK. It's a stage.

GENS. Then it's yours. The theatre of the ghetto. And not just for plays. You can hold meetings, discussions, put on concerts. Here's paper, a pen. Draw up a list of what's missing. Write down anything you need.

SRULIK. By when?

GENS. 'By when?' The day before yesterday. Now!

SRULIK *inspects the building and diffidently draws up his list.*

Scene Four

The ACTOR *who earlier was searching through the pile of clothes, has dressed himself as a* HASSID. *He comes forward.*

HASSID. Your honour! Mr Chief of Police!

GENS. What do you want?

HASSID. I am blessed with a gift. I can foretell your future by means of one glance at your palm. If your honour would oblige me by lending his hand . . .

GENS. Foretelling the future? What rubbish! You've got work to do. Do it!

HASSID. Mister, you don't know what's coming. By summer, your whole life will be revolutionised.

GENS. You know so much? You didn't even look at my palm.

HASSID. I also read ears. The palm gives more detailed results.

GENS *holds out his hand. The* HASSID *examines it.*

HASSID. Amazing!

GENS. What? Tell me.

HASSID. This circle makes a right angle, you see it?

GENS. If you say so.

HASSID. The circle makes the letter 'G'. The right angle an 'L'. Or an 'F'. On your palm a 'G' turns into an 'L'. Or an 'F'.

GENS. Does it mean anything?

HASSID (*looking at his hand*). You are – chief of the Jewish police.

GENS. Fascinating.

HASSID. But that's just the beginning. You're going to run the whole ghetto – 'G'. That's the Germans. You're going to free your people from the Germans. You'll give them their liberty – 'L'. And lead them to freedom – 'F'. See?

GENS (*laughing*). Read the future some more. Tell me when.

The HASSID examines his palm again.

HASSID. In the time of – three cycles.

GENS. Three cycles? What's that?

HASSID. Three weeks, three months, three years.

GENS laughs. The HASSID holds out his hand to be paid.

Three marks.

GENS. What!

HASSID. Three marks, please.

GENS pays, becomes serious.

GENS. Go find some real work. This hocus pocus won't save your life.

The HASSID goes.

Scene Five

GENS (*to* SRULIK). How is the place?

SRULIK. The place is fine. The time isn't.

GENS. It's not?

SRULIK. This is no time to start a theatre.

GENS. Oh.

SRULIK. Three weeks ago fifty thousand Jews were massacred here, right here. Their blood isn't dry! Fifty thousand people, Gens. How can we put on a play?

GENS looks at SRULIK for a moment, walks to a door, opens it.

GENS. You! All of you! Come out of there!

A crowd of women and men enters. They are dressed in rags which look like shrouds. SRULIK, amazed, goes to them. After a moment:

SRULIK. Lionek? Is it you? My God. (*To* OOMA:) Who is this?

GENS. Ooma?

SRULIK. Ooma! (*To* GENS:) Do you know this woman? She was our finest actress. She played Nora. She played Lady Macbeth. Look at her. (*He kisses her.*) Ooma. (SRULIK *lets go of* OOMA.)

GENS *embraces her.*

SRULIK *recognises* HAIKIN.

SRULIK. Haikin! (*He pulls open* HAIKIN*'s ragged coat.* HAIKIN *wears nothing but a filthy cloth.*)

What happened? I searched for you till my eyes came out. (*To* GENS:) This skeleton was leader of the Vilna orchestra for sixteen years. Aron! Gustaw! Miriam! Where did you find them?

GENS. In gutters, in cellars, in forced labour gangs.

HAYYAH *runs on.*

HAYYAH. Haikin! You're alive! (*She embraces him, weeps.*) Haikin! Where's your violin? Somebody give him a violin! Can you play? You must!

One of the actors gives HAIKIN *a violin.* HAYYAH *rubs his hands. Other actors pick up various musical instruments.*

Come, please, darling. There, now your hands are warm. Play!

Hesitantly, HAIKIN *starts to play. Gradually other musicians join in what becomes a tango.*
When the music is over, the actors and musicians return to their pitiful, depressed state.

GENS. Do you know what your friends have in common?

SRULIK. They're all marvellous artists!

GENS. They haven't got work permits. That's all. In the next massacre, they're for the chop. You intellectuals! When all this is over, you'll tell the world: 'Three weeks after the massacre, Gens made us act in a play. I kept my hands clean!' Look in their eyes! Do a play, any play, find parts for them. Give them a job! If they're employed I can get them work permits. And bread. Some butter. Potatoes. Soap.

ALL (*whispering*). Bread. Butter. Potatoes. Soap.

GENS. And that's not all. There's the moral aspect too. We live in dark times. Shouldn't Jewish actors, Jewish musicians use their skills to shed some light? Look at who's next to you. Look at yourselves. You're dejected, depressed. You've lost all will to live. We've forgotten that we're human beings with a language, a culture, a great heritage. Your task is: remind us what we are. I want a performance. Start work.

SRULIK. But what kind of performance? What kind of a theatre?

GENS. Do I ask you how to run a ghetto? Do something that makes us feel human. I ask nothing more.

The actors leave with SRULIK. WEISKOPF *has been amongst the actors. He remains behind with* GENS.

Scene Six

WEISKOPF. Mr Gens! Mr Gens!

GENS. Go with them. Practise your part.

WEISKOPF. I look like an actor?

GENS. Then what are you?

HERMANN KRUK *appears on another part of the stage. He speaks as if dictating to an unseen typist. The sound of a typewriter rattles away in the background.*

KRUK. That's Weiskopf. A few months ago he was a tailor. A face in the crowd. Then – the ghetto. In no time at all he was king. Weiskopf. A name to remember.

WEISKOPF. Spare me only five minutes.

GENS. Three.

WEISKOPF. Mr Gens, you run this ghetto.

GENS. No! The Jewish Council runs the ghetto.

Silence.

Well, in a way. Go on.

WEISKOPF. Mr Gens, have you any idea how many top-class tailors we've got in this place?

GENS. Tailors?

WEISKOPF. How many sewing machines?

GENS. No idea.

WEISKOPF. Look! (*He takes out a note pad and gives it to* GENS.) Tailors, seamstresses, sewing machines. A full list. Names, addresses. I went house to house, room to room.

GENS. But what for?·

WEISKOPF. Mr Gens, can I ask you a question?

GENS. You already have.

WEISKOPF. Mr Gens, at night don't you ever watch the trains going home to Germany all the way from the Russian front?

GENS. Two minutes.

WEISKOPF. What's on those trains? The torn, blood-stained uniforms of the German army. Here's my question. Why do they go back to Germany?

GENS. To be mended.

WEISKOPF. To be mended, to be laundered, to be ironed. Then they send them all the way back. And sitting right in the middle are our tailors, our seamstresses, our sewing machines.

GENS (*examining* WEISKOPF's *note pad*). Enough for a workshop . . .

WEISKOPF. No more *schlepping* uniforms backwards and forwards, wasting coal, blocking railways. The Germans should bring them here! It's good for them, it's good for us.

GENS. How many workers can you use?

WEISKOPF. On day one, a hundred. If it goes well, increase by fifty per cent.

GENS. One hundred and fifty more families saved. My office, tomorrow, eight o'clock.

WEISKOPF. And waste a whole night? No, at eight o'clock you'll take the Germans tables, precise figures, all the details. At ten they'll issue a permit to open a workshop. At twelve we'll start our first shift of the day and we'll take our first tea-break at three.

GENS. My friend, if everyone in the ghetto was like you –

WEISKOPF. Hey! My name's Weiskopf.

GENS. Workshop manager Weiskopf. After you.

GENS ushers him out.

Scene Seven

As KRUK *dictates, the typewriter rattles away. He sorts out some papers.*

KRUK. Weiskopf. In my chronicle of life in the ghetto, he could fill a whole chapter. So could Gens.

He reads from an invitation.

'January the seventeenth, 1942. On Sunday the eighteenth, you are invited to the first performance of the Ghetto Theatre Group. A programme of scenes from plays, satirical songs, modern music, dances.'

Silence.

Write this in capital letters: 'No theatre in a graveyard!'

Members of the ghetto's underground resistance rush on and cover the walls with posters bearing the slogans: 'No theatre in a graveyard!' and 'Don't dance on our graves!' They go off.

Scene Eight

GENS *enters* KRUK's *office holding one of the posters.*

GENS. Hermann Kruk! I know everything that goes on here. What's the meaning of this?

KRUK *holds up the invitation.*

KRUK. I could ask you the same.

GENS. The Theatre Group sent one to every VIP. You're director of the library. Of course you're invited.

KRUK. They think I need entertainment?

GENS. You don't enjoy theatre?

KRUK. You really can't feel how offensive this is?

GENS. Who's offended?

KRUK. I am. So is every other member of the workers' association. In other ghettos perhaps it's still possible to have fun. If there's a chance to do something artistic, meaningful, why not? Go ahead. But in this one? Gens, at Ponar, five miles up the road, there's a pit overflowing with bodies. For God's sake! There were seventy-six thousand Jews in Vilna. How many are left? Fifteen.

GENS. Sixteen!

KRUK. A theatre?

GENS. Hermann Kruk, permit me to remind you of a few facts. September the sixth, 1941. That is, four months ago. No, I'm going to go on. We Jews of Vilna were herded like animals out of our homes, driven here. It was a night spent in hell. Choking with rain, people hauled themselves on hands and knees through the mud. But all you could see were the books flapping in the wind, being kicked about on the ground. You dashed here, there, gathered them up. People who'd lost everything stumbled in a daze through the storm. You rescued pamphlets. The very next morning you opened this library. And for that, though you're a member of the socialist Bund, I salute you. (*He salutes.*)

KRUK. Please . . .

GENS. I disgust you? I don't ask you to salute me. I don't belong to your party. I'm a Zionist. On that black night I didn't notice the books, I admit it. I gathered up women and men. I clothed them. I fed them. I gave them back their professions, their old lives. If they were actors, why shouldn't they act? Haikin, you remember him, must he crush his fingers swinging an axe or should he play his fiddle? You call that a sin? Tomorrow you'll be at the theatre. I insist.

KRUK. Why does it matter to you if we're there or not?

GENS. I want the people to feel solidarity. We're a nation. We must never forget that. Representatives of every group in the ghetto will be there.

KRUK. Why should you miss us? You've invited the chiefs of the Jewish police, the heads of the labour brigades. And such guests: German officers, their gorgeous females. I hear our greatest singer is learning some *lieder* in case they feel homesick.

GENS. We can continue this after the show. Tomorrow you'll come.

KRUK. The workers' association of the ghetto declines your most kind invitation. We won't join your chorus of vultures.

GENS. The workers' association is banned.

KRUK. It's the only democratic organization left in the ghetto!

GENS. You don't say.

KRUK. Your concern for the people, it's hypocrisy! You're building a kingdom! This theatre will be your Versailles! I'll have nothing to do with it!

GENS. You want politics? I'll give you politics. One more poster like this, you and your friends will wake up in Ponar! Don't tempt me!

KRUK (*dictating*). The chief of the ghetto has dissolved the workers' association, the only democratically elected body left in the ghetto because it's 'political'.

GENS. History will judge us. At the time of catastrophe, who served the Jews better, you and your ideals or me! So go on writing everything down. Put it all in your diary. Record this too. Everything!

He goes.

KRUK. I *am* recording it all. What else can I do? (*He dictates.*) We live in the midst of such horror, no one can see what is happening. No-one will listen. They can't understand. I say if we are doomed to become victims of fascism, our duty is to pick up a pen and write everything down. My diary has to see, has to hear. It must become the mirror and the conscience of this appalling catastrophe, these terrible times.

Scene Nine

While KRUK *was speaking, the actors have appeared. They start to rehearse a mournful song, stopping, beginning again, altering the arrangement, the key and so on. Some of the actors pick it up quickly. Others stand about lost, join in for a bit, drop out again, stand staring into space.*

SONG NUMBER THREE.

WEISKOPF *rushes in.*

WEISKOPF. Girls and boys, why the weeping? Why the whining?

SRULIK. Weiskopf, we're rehearsing.

WEISKOPF. Times are hard? So times are hard. When did Jews have it easy? You tell me. Suffering makes us strong, gives us power. Look at me. I could stand and cry. I've got good reason. Before the war I had a drapery. The war came. So they pushed me in here. My shop? *Kaput!* Could I cry? And how! But did I?

I said to myself: why do they call you Weiskopf? Wise Kopf. So I took my wise Jewish kopf and I said: the shop you lost. Will crying bring it back? My arse. If you lose your head as well, you're done for. Nothing else can save you. And that they can't take, not as long as you're alive.

Next I looked around. Walls. A ghetto. I'm closed in. Can I find an opening? Where? I found it! Before the war I was what? A miserable textile worker. Now? I'm managing a tailor's workshop. In the whole region it's number one. Two months and this head's taken me so far! I've got a hundred and fifty Jews working under me. One hundred and fifty! The Germans place their orders, buy my clothes. It's a gigantic operation!

Each day it's getting bigger. The sun rises, my income rises too. And I don't sit on it. My hands are open! If I make a donation to a cause, I give at least five thousand. I'm generous. And I don't hide it. Why should I? Let everyone see and hear. I want the world to know. I'm not ashamed! I make a living and I let others live. Hundreds of others!

Take my example, boys and girls. I'm nothing special. We Jews have talent, more than any other people. If more of us did what I do and stop that whining and complaining, this ghetto would be productive. The Germans would need us! We'd be an asset. Could they get by without us? No! That way we'd survive!

KITTEL appears out of a pile of clothing holding two large cases. He puts them down and applauds.

KITTEL. Bravo, Weiskopf! Bravo! I love this man. And as long as I love him he'll survive.

He goes to OOMA and slaps her. She falls to the ground.

Why no salute?

Everyone salutes.

You're forgiven, this time. I didn't use the gate. Your lookout had no time to warn you: Kittel's in the ghetto. (*He laughs.*) Watch out! Kittel slides around like a snake. Hide in a tunnel, he'll come up through the floor. Lock yourself in the attic, he'll leap down through the roof.

He points at one of his cases. To SRULIK:

What's in there? Take your time. You'll regret a mistake.

SRULIK. The Schmeisser.

KITTEL opens the case, takes out the gun.

KITTEL. Schmeisser!

He cocks the gun. To HAYYAH:

And in that?

HAYYAH. Saxophone.

KITTEL opens the case and takes out the saxophone.

KITTEL. Saxophone! Schmeisser and saxophone. (*In a threatening tone:*) Why do I love you, Weiskopf?

WEISKOPF. I'm useful.

KITTEL laughs.

I help the war effort.

KITTEL. And who made you so productive?

WEISKOPF. You did.

KITTEL Me? (*He smiles then snarls with rage.*) I can't stand arselickers! (*To SRULIK:*) Why should that be?

SRULIK. You're an artist.

KITTEL. What do artists love?

SRULIK. Beauty.

KITTEL. And?

SRULIK. Goodness.

KITTEL. There you are, Weiskopf, that's why I love you. You're beautiful and good. Your energy! Your vitality! You don't owe me that. All I did was provide the right conditions. Take a walk through the streets of the other Vilna, Lithuanian Vilna, Catholic Vilna. They're not people, they're slugs, they're worms. They're the ones we should stamp on, not you.

So I slither in here. Life! Feverish, frantic! There's such beauty, such goodness in that. Can't you see it? No. People who garden in paradise forget the deserts elsewhere. Your shops! Your cafés! Your theatres! Exhibitions! Concerts! Cabaret! Your sense of style! You've run out of luxuries. What do you do! Shred beetroot, call it caviar. The champagne's exhausted? Don't fret. Try a glass of sauerkraut brine. I love it! Your resilience! It's insane!

(To WEISKOPF:) I made you productive? No! I just brought you on, encouraged your inherent beauty to blossom. And we've only started! This painful cross-fertilisation – German soul with Jewish spirit – where will it lead us? Did you dream you would even come this far?

WEISKOPF. I didn't.

KITTEL (to SRULIK). So what else does an artist love?

SRULIK. Truth?

KITTEL. Without truth no art. Weiskopf, answer from the depths of your profound Jewish spirit. Remember, art is truth! Any distortion – (He picks up the gun.) Tell me, what is the difference between partial liquidation and total liquidation?

WEISKOPF. Kill fifty thousand Jews and not me, that's partial liquidation. Kill me, that's total.

KITTEL. Incredible! All this and they can still make jokes. Humour must be in their genes. (To WEISKOPF:) Forget the Schmeisser! (He throws it down and picks up a pot of black paint and a paint brush. He starts painting the actors' faces black.) I give you my word, when the ghetto is destroyed, I'll push a piano to the gate. As you march to the train, I'll play Schumann: 'Scenes from Childhood', 'Kreisleriana', 'Carnaval', our greatest classics, for you!

Silence.

Nobody asks why I'm here. Musicians! To your places, if you please!

The musicians go to their instruments, pick them up.

Suddenly, out of the blue, I just had to hear Gershwin. Isn't that strange? Those philistines, the 'ministry of culture', banned Gershwin. It's a crime to play jazz. Where can I hear him? Nowhere. Then I remembered: the ghetto jazz band! And your singer! (*He picks up his saxophone.*)

Silence.

Where's the singer who owes me fifty grams of beans?

HAYYAH *steps forward.*

You and Gershwin together, how many grams?

He waves his saxophone.

Swanee!

The band plays 'Swanee', HAYYAH gives a sensuous, sparkling performance – her life depends on it.

SONG NUMBER FOUR.

As they play, KITTEL goes to OOMA, drags her up from the ground and starts to dance with her. The actors join in the dancing. When the music is over:

KITTEL. Thank you. Thank you. For the first time in years I felt joy. Which doesn't mean you can't do better. The choreography was dead. This is jazz! The body should swing free and easy. Like so. (*He demonstrates as he sings a line or two. To* HAYYAH:)

But you really are something. I'd like to hear you try 'Porgy and Bess'. Your performance was worth twenty-five grams. Really, not bad. (*To* WEISKOPF:) You allow my artists to perform in those rags?

WEISKOPF. I offered them costumes.

KITTEL. Then do it! Use the best cloth!

WEISKOPF. Naturally! From the top drawer!

KITTEL. I'll be there to see! (*To the others:*) I'm always here to see.

So watch out! Kittel can creep through any crack, any hole.
Look, it's Kittel! The snake!

He laughs and leaves the way he came.

Scene Ten

*The huge heap of dirty rags has become a neatly stacked pile of mended and
laundered uniforms and clothes.*

WEISKOPF. Costumes . . .? Any size, any style, I've got it. Some
we patched. This blouse has bullet holes. (*He throws it to an
actress.*) Find them. This jacket was ripped from here to here
with a bayonet. This one's brand new. (*He switches them behind his
back.*) Which is which? Don't be nervous!

The actors start to examine the clothing.

Dresses, suits, slips, trousers, tailcoats, overcoats, undershirts. If
you need, take – there's plenty. English corduroy, can you use
it? Fine linen from Naples, French silk, it's gorgeous. Starched,
ironed, everything ready for use. I've got children's clothes,
piles of it. A little girl's skirt. With blue rabbits. Are there any
children in your play?

Appalled, the actors throw back the clothes.

Something's wrong? It's clothing. What else should it be? Here.
Policemen: jacket, trousers, hat, a complete set. Judge's robes,
doctor's gowns – we've got dozens. Hassidic frocks, plenty,
even a rabbi's hat. Tweed suits, the finest from Manchester.
This one was heavy with mud, we got it out.

Ties from Warsaw. Polish uniforms, who needs one? Uniforms
of heroes. Bayonets in hand, on horseback, they charged
German tanks. It didn't do the uniforms much good. Peppered
with bullet holes. My women sewed them up. Is there even a
spot of blood? German uniforms, all ranks, we've got them. We
make no distinctions. Everyone gets treated the same. Into the
laundry!

You should visit our laundry. You'll come out with a show. In
our cauldrons are human dramas. The fires in the ovens roar!
The air weeps tears of soap and chlorine. Everything comes out

in the wash – the mud, the blood, the oil! The sewage boils in black and crimson streams. And then on to the sewing workshop. A gigantic hall. A hundred and fifty sewing machines clanking and rattling. It's like a railway station!
Help yourselves! Why hold back? Clothing, we've got plenty. Yes, clothing's one commodity that's not in short supply.

Some of the actors have picked out costumes. A few have started to put them on. The first to be dressed is JUDITH. *She covers her head with a shawl and – improvising a scene – rushes at* WEISKOPF *who doesn't realise what is going on. He continues sorting through the clothes and offering them to the actors. Other actors watch the improvisation and comment to each other.*

JUDITH. Help me! They've taken my husband! Oh, my husband!

WEISKOPF (*without looking at her*). Don't worry. It'll work out all right.

JUDITH. They caught him buying flour. They took him straight to Lukishki.

WEISKOPF. I told you: don't worry.

JUDITH. Your honour, you're the only one –

WEISKOPF. Not now. I'm busy!

JUDITH. If we can only find twenty thousand roubles, if we can just pay the fine –

WEISKOPF. Who's talking to you? Am I talking to you?

JUDITH. Please, hurry! No-one comes home from Lukishki!

JUDITH addresses some of the other actors who are partly dressed in WEISKOPF'*s clothes.*

This man's an angel. He gives food to the poor. He frees people from jail. We should kiss his white hands. (*To* OOMA:) Are you a doctor?

OOMA (*hesitantly, as if waking from a dream*). What? Oh, yes. A doctor.

OOMA *finishes her dressing by putting on a doctor's black coat. She will play the part of* WEINER, *a young physician.*

JUDITH. Doctor, my husband's diabetic. Help me get him his insulin. Without it he won't live a day.

WEISKOPF. Go home. Make your husband soup. He'll drink it then have insulin for dessert.

JUDITH. That's how he is. He helps everyone. (*To the* RABBI:) Are you a rabbi?

Silence. Then the RABBI *finishes his dressing up by putting on a rabbi's hat.*

Bless him, rabbi, bless him. Pray God keeps him strong.

WEISKOPF. OK, I'm finished. I'll go see my German. Come to my office in one hour. Don't be late! I've got plenty other problems to sort out, not only you.

WEISKOPF *goes.*

The actors gently applaud JUDITH *who takes off her shawl and throws it back onto the pile.* SRULIK *embraces her. Silence. As the actors begin to improvise,* SRULIK *moves the others aside, turning them into an audience and clearing a space for the performance. Then he moves among the actors, encouraging and prompting them. An actor who will play the elderly* DR GOTTLIEB *has put on doctor's clothes. Another actor has dressed as a judge. (These parts, and that of the* RABBI, *may be played by either men or women.)*

Scene Eleven

WEINER. Gentlemen, I've called you to this meeting in the hospital basement for one reason and one reason only.

RABBI. Who are you?

WEINER. Dr Weiner. I am in charge of the hospital dispensary. In the ghetto we have fifty diabetics. Some are serious cases in the final phase of the disease. At any moment they may lapse into unconsciousness. As my colleague, Dr –

GOTTLIEB. Gottlieb!

WEINER. – Dr Gottlieb can verify these patients need high doses of insulin, up to fifty units a day.

RABBI. Fifty injections every day?

GOTTLIEB. No, no, no. Fifty units can be given in three or four doses. (*To* WEINER:) Keep it simple. Stick to the point.

WEINER. How can they advise us if we don't tell them everything?

JUDGE. Some patients need fifty units a day. We understand so much. Go on.

WEINER. Of course other patients are much better off. They can get by with, let's say, ten units. They're young, they're fit. Apart, of course, from their diabetes.

JUDGE It all seems quite logical.

WEINER. Yes, now: to keep all fifty diabetics alive we need one thousand units each day. In my dispensary we have one hundred thousand. Enough for three months. When it's gone, the most seriously ill will be dead within days. The others will take longer. All will die.

GOTTLIEB. So we'll raise money, buy insulin on the black market like we buy other medicines.

GENS enters. The actors stop acting. GENS makes a gesture inviting them to go on. They resume.

WEINER. There is no more insulin.

GENS. That's right.

GOTTLIEB. Not even on the black market?

JUDGE. Nonsense! You can buy anything – French soap, perfume – if you can meet the price.

GENS. Forget it.

WEINER. There's none. Not anywhere in the whole city.

GENS. Nor in any other ghetto.

WEINER. In fact, we're well off. If the Germans knew how much we have, they'd take the lot. We haven't even told them we have any diabetics. No, for once it's not a question of price. Insulin is priceless. There's none to be had.

JUDGE. So what are you asking us? What can we do?

WEINER. Well, if we stop treating the serious cases, we'd need four hundred units a day instead of a thousand. Our supply would last nine months. If we're even more rigorous in choosing who we treat, we can keep the twenty most healthy alive for a year and a half, maybe two.

RABBI. This is ridiculous. It's crazy to plan even two months ahead. God knows what could happen. Even two days!

JUDGE. He's right. For us two months is eternity. You say we have insulin for three.

WEINER. That isn't the point.

JUDGE. The point is that I'm not a doctor. Neither is he. How can we tell if this one is critical or that one? We can't advise you which patients to treat.

WEINER. That's not what I'm asking you!

JUDGE. So explain.

WEINER. My question is: do I have the moral right to stop treating the seriously ill, to let them die so that others will have a better chance to pull through?

Silence. It becomes more and more oppressive.

JUDGE. Presumably you invited me here because I'm a judge. Very well. Let's consider the case from a legal viewpoint. We start with the general case. Do we ever have the right to sentence people to death? Answer: we do. We may execute those convicted of certain crimes provided the law stipulates the death sentence. We move on to the particular. Of which crime are you accusing these people? If I understand you, their crime is that they are seriously ill. What's the evidence? Does it stand up? You've measured the level of their blood sugar and so on and so on. Now I must tell you I have read, I won't say every law book but, in my life, quite a few. I have never found it written that possessing a blood sugar level of any degree is grounds for passing the death sentence. Never. So, madam prosecutor, I can inform you there are no grounds in law that allow me to sanction the execution of these people.

WEINER. Juridicially you may be right. But I'm appalled at the casual way in which you condemn every one of these people. Rabbi, I need guidance.

Silence.

RABBI. A story from the Talmud. Will it help? It can't hurt. So let's try. An army is besieging a city. They demand as the price for lifting the siege . . . thirty people. If they're handed over to be slaughtered, the city will be spared. I'm not saying it fits our case exactly. Let's see where it gets us. So the Talmud asks:

should we hand over the thirty or not? And the Talmud answers: if no individuals have been specified you must hand over no-one. The whole city must go up in flames. But if the enemy asks: give us this one and this one, if they ask for them by name, then hand them over, save everyone else. So says the Talmud. Now, who here is the enemy? Can anyone specify which individuals must die so that others may live? Obviously not.

WEINER. Here is the list. Patients and case histories, patients and blood sugar levels, patients and marital status, age, profession. What more do you need?

RABBI. I don't want to look at it.

JUDGE. Nor do I. Put it away!

WEINER (*reading*). Seventy-eight, widower, no children, critical. You want his name? Thirty-six, married, father of three –

GOTTLIEB. How dare you do this?

RABBI. Only God can give life. Only he can take it. Human beings have no right to interfere.

KITTEL *appears out of nowhere and gets on the stage. The actors freeze.*

KITTEL. Gens! Gens!

GENS *comes on.*

I need help with a problem of logic. A man and wife have a child. Have they increased the race or not?

GENS. They haven't.

KITTEL. And if they have two children?

GENS. Still no. Two children from two parents is no increase.

KITTEL. Three children?

GENS. They've increased.

KITTEL. Is that so? So we do have a problem. The Führer has forbidden any increase of the Jewish race. One child, fine. Two, still permissible. Three?

GENS. One too many.

KITTEL. You've solved my problem! I knew you would. OK, let's do it.

GENS. Do what?

KITTEL. Get rid of every third child.

He throws a stick to GENS.

Father, mother, child, child. The third one – (*Snaps his fingers.*)

Using the stick, GENS *carries out the selection.*

GENS. Father, mother, child, child . . . Father, mother, child, child . . . Get a move on! Hurry it up! Father, mother, child, child . . . Move faster!

KRUK *appears. He speaks against a background of* GENS's *selection, the screaming of the families, the rattling of his typewriter. After a moment the sound of screaming is transferred into song.*

SONG NUMBER FIVE.

KRUK. A father, a wife and three children. Gens counts them: Father, mother, child, child. The third child is a twelve year-old boy. He's shoved out of line, hit on the back with the stick. Mother, father, child, child are pushed into the group of survivors. They cry: 'It's a Jew who's taken our child from us!' The crowd starts to murmur then to scream: 'Gens is a traitor! Gens is killing our children!' Gens pays no attention: Father, mother, child, child. Father, mother, child. A family with only one child. Gens yells at the father: 'You idiot! What have you done with your second child?' The father, already distraught, becomes terrified. 'I only have one!' Gens lashes at him with his stick. 'Imbecile! Where is your other child?' In all the confusion, nobody sees Gens retrieve the twelve-year-old boy with his stick, thrust him into the arms of the man. 'Here he is! Here is your second child. Hold onto him. Next time you'll lose him for good.' Father, mother, child, child. The boy, almost fainting, stands among strangers, among the survivors. Two hundred and nineteen others were sent to Ponar.

KRUK *goes.* GENS, KITTEL, *the families have gone. Some of the actors – not* WEINER *– have taken off part of their costumes. The argument continues for real between them.*

RABBI. No one has the moral authority to decide who will live, who will die. Only God gives life. Only he can take it away.

WEINER. In what world? A world in which justice prevails. Here? Here men decide everything. The will of God? It's the will of evil men.

RABBI. That's blasphemy.

WEINER. We all cling to vague hopes. The Russians will break through. Our families, our friends will survive. Maybe, maybe. In this liquid you can see hope, you can touch it. For some this is life. God's will? No, it's your will. It's mine.

RABBI. Blasphemy!

WEINER (*to* GOTTLIEB) You're older, more experienced than I am. Say something. Help me.

GOTTLIEB. Discriminating between patients? There's never any justification. I'm leaving this meeting in protest.

(*He throws his costume on the pile, goes out.*)

WEINER. So I must dole it out, first come first served? Blindly, mechanically with no thought, no feeling, no plan?

RABBI. You with your direct access to the almighty, do as you please!

JUDGE. Selecting patients to live or to die? That's Nazi medicine!

RABBI *and* JUDGE *throw their costumes back on the pile, go out. The other actors and* SRULIK *have gone.*

WEINER. Let everyone perish! Avoid the moral issues! You're the Nazi doctors not me!

Scene Twelve

GENS *returns to the deserted theatre with a bottle in his hand. He is drunk and exhausted.*

GENS. Father, mother, child, child. Father, mother . . . (*He sees* OOMA.) Still here? (*He flings himself down on the pile of clothing.*) You've got papers, fake Polish papers. Don't deny it, I know you have. And the right face. Your accent's pure Warsaw. What are you waiting for? Leave the ghetto.

OOMA. I'm afraid.

GENS. You'd be safer with the partisans in the forest.

OOMA. I'm afraid to make a decision. To break out, to fight, to resist – that takes courage. To stay, even to die, that's nothing.

GENS. I can't understand you.

OOMA. To live here – it's just something that happened to me. To resist – who knows, maybe it's not the right time. We've lived through so many disasters. Make a decision? On what grounds? In fact I made a decision, we all did: wait and see.

GENS. There's no future for the ghetto.

OOMA. You served in the Lithuanian army.

GENS. So?

OOMA. You understand weapons. Why don't you go to the forest?

GENS. I belong here with my people.

OOMA. They need you to fight!

As he speaks, GENS *recovers from his drunkenness.*

GENS. They still don't see what's being done to them. Listen! There is another kind of resistance. Not fighting, not the forest, not even joining the underground here in this ghetto. OK, pretend you don't know what goes on. You're all mixed up in it. I know everything! No! Real resistance is deeper. And harder. And has to be done!

You asked me a question. 'Why don't I go to the forest?' I'll tell you. The Germans want to destroy us. Physically yes, but worse than that, spiritually. They want to cut out our souls. Can we resist? They've conquered all Europe. Can we fight them? Only on the spiritual level. 'Neither by might, nor by power, but by our spirit, saith the Lord!' Do you hear?

That insulin. Let me tell you about it. Jews have always suffered, always. Never like this. They want to kill us all. Listen: all. They won't. No, no, they're going to lose this war. But when they've retreated, gone, what state will our souls be in? Pure, Jewish, healthy? Or riddled with their fatal disease?

We must build a wall round our souls. In this spiritual ghetto we'll protect who? You don't know? The strong. That's what that insulin means. Protect the strong! In body, in spirit. Do you see what we've come to? Selection! That's it. The sick, the weak, the hopeless – (*Snaps his fingers.*) What else can we do? (*He drinks.*)

Will our grandchildren understand why we did it? Will they

justify us in their songs, in their plays? Who cares! We must save what we can. So I won't go to the forest. My work is here. I want theatre. And lectures. Education. Intellectual activities. I must save as many Jews as I can! (*He drinks.*) There's no future in the ghetto. (*He drinks.*) None at all.

GENS *collapses.* OOMA, *who is sitting on the ground, takes him in her lap and sings a lullaby.*

SONG NUMBER SIX.

Fade out.

End of Part One.

PART TWO

Prologue

Members of the company form a human chain. They throw German uniforms from one to another and pile them into a huge heap. As they work they sing 'Yiddishe Brigades'.

SONG NUMBER SEVEN.

Scene Thirteen

Night. Four young people, three men and a woman, climb through a hole in the ghetto wall carrying a coffin. GENS *appears, shines his torch on them.*

GENS. Luba Grodzenski!

LUBA. Who wants her?

GENS (*of the coffin*). What's that?

LUBA. Someone died. We took him out, buried him. We can't waste a coffin.

GENS. But why through a hole in the wall? What's wrong with the gate?

GEIVISH. This way – it's quicker.

GENS. If you bastards are smuggling weapons –

LUBA. Weapons?

GEIVISH. For who?

YANKEL. He thinks we belong to the underground!

All four laugh.

GENS. Belong? No, you don't have the guts to join anything. But you'd supply them.

LUBA. We don't, chief. I swear it.

GENS. Then what are you smuggling? Hungarian salami? Sugar? Coffee?

YANKEL. Nothing! God strike me if I'm lying!

LUBA. The ghost of the dead, chief. That's all.

GENS. His sins weigh very heavy. Tomorrow nine a.m., my office. You'll give five thousand roubles to the school for delinquents.

GEIVISH. Five?

LUBA. It's usually three.

GENS. Five, damn you! Right, come, pay it now.

LUBA. Tomorrow nine a.m. Five. I swear it.

GENS *grabs* LUBA.

GENS. She'll sit in my office till you pay! Jacob Gens can be pushed only so far.

GENS *pushes* LUBA *out.*

ELIA. And now?

YANKEL. We can't let her sweat all night.

GEIVISH. And the five thousand? It will fall from the sky?

YANKEL. I can't just stand here.

GEIVISH. Just stand there. Weiskopf will come, fetch his order, pay what he owes. We give Gens his tax and she's free.

ELIA. And now?

Silence. Then ELIA *starts to sing.*

SONG NUMBER EIGHT.

YANKEL. Hey! Someone's there.

The HASSID *comes on.*

GEIVISH. Are you from Weiskopf?

HASSID. Good evening.

YANKEL. Him!

GEIVISH. Are you working for Weiskopf?

HASSID. Me? I'm a reader of palms.

YANKEL. Piss off!

HASSID. Mister, you don't know what's coming. By next summer, your whole life will be revolutionised.

GEIVISH. He said –

ELIA. Wait. (*To the* HASSID:) How do you know that? You haven't even looked at his palm.

HASSID. I also read ears. The palm gives more detailed results.

ELIA. Is that so?

He holds out his hand. The HASSID *looks at it.*

HASSID. So, what do we find here? This circle makes a right angle, you see it?

ELIA. Go on.

HASSID. The circle makes the letter 'G'. The right angle an 'F'. On your palm a 'G' turns into an 'F'. 'G' stands for Germans. 'F' for Freedom. In the time of three we'll be free of the Germans!

ELIA. What the hell is the time of three?

HASSID. Three weeks, three months, three years. Twenty roubles. (*He holds out his hand.*)

ELIA. How about three seconds?

HASSID. Fine. Thirty roubles.

ELIA *draws a knife with his right hand.*

ELIA. OK. One, two, three.

He stabs the HASSID. *The* HASSID *falls.* ELIA *pulls out the knife, goes through the* HASSID's *pockets.*

GEIVISH. Are you insane?

YANKEL. Why the hell did you do that?

ELIA *counts money he's taken from the* HASSID.

ELIA. One thousand, three thousand, here's our five thousand!

GEIVISH (*of the coffin*). Empty this, put him in.

They open the coffin. A figure wrapped in shrouds sits up, then stands.

The three men are terrified. They run off. The dead man gets out of the coffin and starts removing his shrouds. KRUK *enters. As he dictates, the unseen typewriter rattles away.*

KRUK. For the second time a murder has been committed in the ghetto for the sake of money. I've found out what I can. Both crimes were tied up with our flourishing blackmarket. Our rich splash out on every kind of luxury the underworld mob can provide.

He sits and writes.

Scene Fourteen

When the dead man removes the last of his shrouds he is revealed to be KITTEL. *He takes a few thick books from the coffin, puts glasses on his nose and becomes* DR PAUL, *a professor of Judaica.*

PAUL. Do I have the honour of addressing Mr Hermann Kruk?

KRUK. With whom have I the pleasure?

PAUL. Dr Ernst Paul. From the Rosenberg Institute for the Study of Judaism without Jews. You know of our researches?

KRUK. Vaguely . . .

PAUL. We have a mission. To analyse and document the spiritual and intellectual components of the Jewish cultural experience. We gain entry for our scholars to selected field sites. This is one. If anything of outstanding merit is uncovered – what we term cultural assets: songs, embroidery, religious artefacts, literature – these are deposited at our Institute recently established in Frankfurt. Our hope is to complete our investigation before all bearers of this complex heritage are, *hélas*, taken from us. I am sure you and I will quickly develop the mutual trust and respect scholars habitually enjoy. I see you've never heard of me. I'm prepared for that. All my published works.

He hands his books to KRUK. KRUK *pages through one.*

KRUK. Commentaries on the Talmud . . .?

PAUL. The Jerusalem Talmud is my particular study.

KRUK. How did you find me?

PAUL. By the opposite route to that used by Rabbi Yochanan ben Zakkai.

KRUK. You'll have to explain.

PAUL. Ah? I thought . . . When the besieged city of Jerusalem was on the point of destruction, four of the rabbi's disciples put him in a coffin and smuggled him out. When I wished to enter your Jerusalem, I used the same means to be smuggled in.

He laughs. Silence.

But perhaps you don't like to use German. We can speak Yiddish. Or Hebrew.

KRUK. My language is Yiddish.

PAUL. Fine! Both Hebrew and German are so formal, don't you find? As the wise man said: Hebrew you talk, Yiddish talks itself. Let's try to relax.

They sit.

KRUK. I'd like to ask, how . . .

PAUL. Did I, a non-Jew, learn Yiddish? Is that it? Or did you think I was Jewish? Even in Palestine they thought so. At the time of the Arab revolts I was there on a mission. A bunch of Arab bandits tried to throttle me. Jewish underground fighters chanced by – strong, lively fellows – or we wouldn't be sitting here now.

He laughs in an abrupt frightening manner, then snaps back into his usual sombre mood as if his laughter had been cut off with a knife.

Of course you know Jerusalem.

KRUK. No.

PAUL. A grave loss.

KRUK. I've never set foot in Palestine. I'm not a Zionist.

PAUL. Rather a communist.

KRUK *looks at* PAUL. *He realises* PAUL *knows everything.*

KRUK. That's a long time ago.

PAUL. Are you ashamed to recall it?

KRUK. 'Ashamed'. (*He thinks about this.*) At that time, the October Revolution, I was wild with excitement. Anticipation! I believed

– we all believed – justice, universal justice, the end of persecution of all minorities, even we Jews . . . Ashamed? Not at all!

PAUL. But you resigned from the party. Why? The Stalinist terrors?

KRUK. Not at all. I resigned years before! No, it wasn't Stalin who drove me out of the party. It was the Jews. They were so quick with criticism, no, worse, contempt for their own people's culture, literature, philosophy. They mocked their fathers' language, their fathers' beliefs.

PAUL. So you were religious?

KRUK. I'll rot in the earth and that's the end of it. None of us were, few of us are. But I couldn't come to terms with their scorn. Until now.

PAUL. Now?

KRUK. Now I have. Thanks to you.

PAUL. Me?

KRUK. You Germans.

PAUL. Now *you'll* have to explain.

KRUK. Jacob Gens, a Jew, carries out the orders of the Germans, rules this ghetto. Dessler, a Jew, is the local agent of the Gestapo. Levas, a Jew, guards the main ghetto gate, keeps us imprisoned. Who can be trusted to beat Jews most brutally? I could write you a list. All Jews. The Jewish Council, charged with administering our day to day lives, their office – it's a pit, debauchery, corruption. Our Jewish police drink with your officers, crawl onto their beds, share their Jewish whores. Why do we hate ourselves? Why? Oppression, two thousand years. It does great damage. I see that now. Thanks to you.

PAUL. And seeing all that, you still belong to the Bund?

KRUK. Go on.

PAUL. Well, sitting where we are, can you really imagine a socialist state here in Europe where Jews will be equal and free?

KRUK. If I'll see it, I don't know. It will come.

PAUL. There's a Hassidic legend. Once there was a king. One day he flew into a rage with his son and threw him out of the

palace. Time went by. The king's heart grew cool. He shouted
for one of his servants. 'Go find my son. Tell him he has three
wishes. Come back, tell me what they are.' The servant travelled
and searched. At last he found the prince. He'd grown thin. He
had filthy rags on his back. He slept on the ground by an open
sewer. The servant woke him. 'If a king offered you three
wishes, what would they be?' The prince replied without
thinking: 'Bread, clothes, a roof over my head.' When the king
heard this he fell to his knees and wailed. 'My son is lost
forever.' You see, if he'd remembered who he was he'd have
made only one wish, to return to the palace. Everything he
could want would be there. You dream of – what? Cultural
autonomy. A bill of rights. Why not return to the palace? In
Palestine you'd have everything now, not at the millenium
when good triumphs over evil.

KRUK. You're recruiting for Zionism?

PAUL. Mr Kruk, you say you despise the way Gens uses Jews as
police.

KRUK. He makes the best of the situation you put him in.

PAUL. Why defend him? Or his cronies? I don't. I can't bear to
look at them. They imitate us but they fail. Repulsive
fairground caricatures. But we heard that you weren't like that.
You've kept your integrity, your courage. So we're prepared to
drop Gens, appoint you. You run the ghetto.

Silence.

KRUK. Take power from you? It's not possible.

PAUL. So you'd rather have Gens?

KRUK. In your legend, it seems to me that what the prince
understood is what's crucial and what's not. It's not power that
matters.

PAUL. So you'll stay in the diaspora powerless and leave Zion,
leave Palestine to the likes of Gens who'll grab it with both
brutish hands? You're just like the Jews you despise. You too
hate yourself.

KRUK. Wherever I live my culture is my homeland. Betray your
culture, in your own home you're an exile. Then it's one step
from humanism to nationalism. One more? Bestiality. I'll stay
as I am.

PAUL *stands, takes a list from his pocket.*

PAUL. This selection of manuscripts is required for the Frankfurt Institute.

He gives the list to KRUK.

I want them packed and ready by morning. We'll talk more another time.

The noise of a crowd. GENS, *a judge and a doctor come on.* GEIVISH, ELIA *and* YANKEL, *their hands tied, are led in.*

PAUL. Look! The other Jews. Our Jews. The damaged who understand power!

He laughs in his characteristic way and disappears.

Scene Fifteen

When the JUDGE, *the prisoners and the others have entered, men in butchers' clothes bring in two large wooden frames, each ten foot high, with meat hooks inserted into their upper cross pieces. Three nooses are dangling from the hooks. Three chairs are placed against the frames. A rope is attached to each chair. While this is happening,* GENS *speaks:*

GENS. Your Honour!

JUDGE. On June the fourth, 1942, the Jewish court of the Vilna ghetto heard the case of Yankel Polikanski and the brothers Yitzhak and Elia Geivish, hereafter known as the defendants. The charges against them were as follows: that on the night of June the third they stabbed to death one Yosef Gerstein. In addition it was revealed to the court that the defendants had also murdered one Herzl Liedes who was found buried in a basement in Strashun Street. On both counts the defendants were found guilty and sentenced to be hanged by the neck.

KITTEL *appears and stands near* GENS. *They salute each other.*

GENS. Your honours, members of the Jewish Council of the ghetto, officers of the police, Ladies and Gentlemen. At one time in Vilna there were seventy-five thousand Jews. Now there's sixteen. It is the duty of you sixteen thousand to live honest lives, to work hard. If you fail, you will suffer the same fate as these three, these Jews who took the lives of fellow Jews. Our Jewish police will string you up with their own Jewish hands. *A group of actors including* JUDITH *and* OOMA *start to sing* 'Isrulik'. *The crowd joing in.*

SONG NUMBER EIGHT.

When the song is finished, GENS *orders:-*

GENS. Begin!

Two policemen escort the three to the scaffold. They climb onto the chairs, Nooses are placed around their necks. GENS *raises a stick, gives a signal. The ropes are pulled, the chairs come away, the three are hanged.*

KRUK. One of the ropes broke. Yankel Polikanski fell to the ground. Gens wanted to free him. Kittel turned his thumb down. Pick up the chair, prepare a new rope. This time it didn't fail.

In the centre of the stage, KITTEL *takes out a letter sealed with wax, breaks the seal, reads:*

KITTEL. We have just witnessed the inception of autonomous and responsible Jewish government in the Vilna ghetto. Whereas the present Jewish Council has failed in its duties, requiring for even the simplest decision time-wasting discussion and vote after vote after vote, the Jewish Council is hereby dissolved. Whereas for all practical purposes Mr Jacob Gens has been running the ghetto for some considerable time, in recognition of his dedication and efficiency I hereby appoint Mr Jacob Gens ruler of the ghetto.

Applause.

His assistant will be Mr Fried.

Applause.

Replacing Mr Gens as chief of police will be Mr Dessler.

Applause.

GENS. I assure you I will do everything in my power to serve my people as best as I can. All senior police officers, dignitaries and officials are invited to a ball.

KITTEL. Thanks for inviting me. I'd love to come provided there's music and cabaret.

GENS. I'll see to it.

KITTEL. And your wonderful singer? She owes me a song. Tonight seems the right time to pay. (*He is about to go, stops.*) In your honour, I give permission to bring flowers into the ghetto. (*He goes. The jazz band enters playing sentimental music. The bodies and scaffolds are removed.*)

Scene Sixteen

The stage is filled with actors who decorate it with large bouquets of flowers. Rugs and cushions create an atmosphere of ease and relaxation. Large quantities of refreshments – wine, salamis, roast chickens – are brought in and displayed. WEISKOPF comes in, runs up and down, supervising the preparations.

WEISKOPF. Where are the flowers? Bring more flowers! I want the room full of flowers. No! This is the cold meats buffet. Roast chickens over there. Wait! The sauce, does it go on the chicken? Then it goes by the chicken. And the *cholent*? Where's the *cholent*? Yes, we want it when everyone's gone home. Bring it! Idiot.

Bottles over there. No. Put bottles all over. Make it easy to find a bottle. Open them. All of them! Every single bottle! Don't fuss about what's left over. It goes to charity.

We'll show them a Jewish celebration. We'll show those swine! The *kvass* here! I said open them all! Are you trying to save me money? Why? Does it belong to your father? It's mine. I'm going to make such a deal with them what I spend today I'll make back tomorrow ten times, fifty times!

More actors and musicians come in.

The orchestra is here! Where's the stage? Oh. Fine. The stage is ready. That's how you decorate a stage? Put on flowers! Lots of flowers! Make their eyes pop out their sockets, run into their cheeks. That's it. More flowers! Let them see what a Jew is made of. Take their breath away.

I wish them every one of Pharaoh's plagues. Yes, and Job's leprosy. Arrange the meat so it looks nice. They'll take a look and stuff themselves. I hope they choke! I hope their tongues grow boils! Let them eat till they're stuffed, till they're blocked up front and back. Shit it out. They can't. It won't budge.

They're stuffed up good and solid but they can't stop shoving it in.

Rice by the meat, potatoes by the rice. I want them bursting with shit! Let them fart out their guts and tie them in knots round their necks. That's beautiful! Beautiful! So, are we ready? Orchestra, music. One and two and three!

The orchestra plays. Guests enter. GENS, DESSLER – who is fat and bald with a thick black moustache – Jewish members of the ghetto police, KITTEL, Gestapo officers, Jewish prostitutes come in half drunk, singing a German song: 'Ich bin di fesche Lola'. SRULIK and his DUMMY and HAYYAH wearing a beautiful evening gown. WEISKOPF greets them and offers them an aperitif and hors d'oeuvres.

As they eat HAYYAH sings.

SONG NUMBER NINE.

While HAYYAH is singing, the orgy begins. Sex is only between the Jewish police and the prostitutes. Most of the Germans watch. One or two take girls behind a curtain or under a table. When the singing ends, the audience applauds. KITTEL raises his hand. Silence. He goes to HAYYAH, takes her hand, kisses it. Applause. KITTEL raises his hand again.

KITTEL (*to HAYYAH*). Close your eyes.

She does. He produces a long string of pearls, shows it to the guests. They gasp. He puts the pearls on HAYYAH's neck.

Open.

HAYYAH opens her eyes and is appalled by the pearls.

KITTEL. They're only pearls, I'm afraid. But if you knew where they come from . . .

HAYYAH tries to pull off the pearls. KITTEL stops her.

You wear their shoes, why not their pearls? Keep them. That song – ten grams. You still owe fifteen.

DUMMY. Ten grams? That's all you're worth now.

KITTEL goes to the DUMMY.

KITTEL. Our funny little friend. Still sticking out your neck?

DUMMY. Just my tongue. It's my Jewish *hutzpah*.

KITTEL. Give me an example of Jewish *hutzpah*, if you've got the nerve.

DUMMY. Not now.

KITTEL. Why's that?

DUMMY. You don't look well.

KITTEL. It's true. I've got rather a headache.

DUMMY. Take a sequence of head baths. You'll never suffer again.

KITTEL. A sequence of head baths?

DUMMY. Yes! The sequence is: put your head in water three times, take it out twice.

KITTEL *laughs. Everyone else interrupts the orgy to laugh as well. He signals them to stop. They do, holding their breath. Suddenly* KITTEL *laughs again.*

DUMMY. Do you know why Germans laugh at jokes twice?

KITTEL. Tell me.

DUMMY. The first time: politeness. The second: they've just got the point.

KITTEL *laughs, falls silent, laughs again, falls silent again.*

KITTEL. And that's as far as you're prepared to go?

DUMMY. Uh uh.

KITTEL. I bet it is.

DUMMY. How much?

SRULIK (*to the* DUMMY). That's enough.

DUMMY. He wants to gamble. It's my head on the block. (*To* KITTEL:) Your stake: fifty thousand.

KITTEL *pulls out a banknote.*

KITTEL. I've only got one.

WEISKOPF *appears beside* KITTEL *with a stack of notes.*

WEISKOPF. Mr Kittel, be my guest.

KITTEL. Who's got a pen? I'll sign a receipt.

WEISKOPF *searches for a pen.*

DUMMY. What for? We all know Germans are honest. After all, you took Leningrad, you gave it back. You took Stalingrad, you gave it back. You'll pay him back, penny for penny.

KITTEL *is stunned into silence. Everyone else is silent too.*

KITTEL *holds out* WEISKOPF's *money to* SRULIK.

KITTEL. You win.

SRULIK *splutters, tries to hand the money back to* KITTEL.

SRULIK. No! Keep it! Please!

KITTEL *has already turned away.*

DUMMY (*to* SRULIK). Fool! To steal from a thief isn't stealing.

KITTEL (*to* SRULIK). Enough! (*He shakes the* DUMMY.)

WEISKOPF. Mr Kittel, have you sampled my cognac? It's first-class French.

He gives KITTEL *a glass. They both throw off their drinks in one gulp.*

KITTEL. Ahhh! Paris . . . Paris . . .

The orchestra plays a French song. HAYYAH *sings.*

SONG NUMBER TEN.

While they sing, WEISKOPF *leads* KITTEL *a short distance away.*

WEISKOPF. Mr Kittel, have I got an offer to make you.

As he talks to KITTEL, *the orgy and the singing continue. One of the German officers gets carried away, pulls a prostitute from one of the Jewish policemen and attempts to enjoy her himself. Another German officer quickly separates them, threatens the German, pushes the prostitute back to the Jew. The Germans continue to enjoy the orgy as observers. When the song is over,* WEISKOPF *claps for silence.*

WEISKOPF. Ladies and gentlemen! Have I got news! Mr Kittel and I have just hammered out the fine points of the biggest deal in the history of our factory. Four hundred railcars of uniforms! Four hundred! Which means work for you all! And there's more. I've been given a promise, I can't say from who, of a meeting with Göring. In Berlin. I will personally negotiate with Mr Göring a five year contract. Manufacturing, mending – uniforms, fatigues, combat boots. We'll build a new plant.

Whatever they want from us, we'll turn it out. So, my friends, it's a happy day. Fill your glasses! *Lehayim!*

SONG NUMBER ELEVEN.

During the song, the drinking and the orgy grow more frenzied.

KITTEL. Gens. Gens!

GENS goes to KITTEL who puts his hand on his shoulder and walks up and down with him.

You're not enjoying yourself?

GENS. I am. Immensely.

KITTEL. Dessler is having a good time. Mushkat is having a good time. Look at Levas. He's having a good time. You don't enjoy parties. Organise them, OK, no problem. But enjoy them? You can't. Why? You can't stop calculating. Your eye's always peeled. A party's just a chance to work a whole roomful of us at the same time. Something from this one, something from that. I can't stand it. If you don't relax I can't. Be happy, Gens. Won't you? For me. (*Sings:*) 'I want to be happy but I can't be happy till I make you happy too.'

GENS. I'll try.

KITTEL. I'll give you a hand.

He raises his hand. Silence.

Gentlemen. Ladies. I wish to inform you of an expansion in the empire of our good friend Gens. From this moment, the ghetto at Oshmene is annexed to this one. Mr Gens, with the help of the Jewish police and the revered Mr Dessler, you are now the ruler of the Jews of Oshmene as well.

Applause. DESSLER stands, takes a bow. Silence.

Inevitably, there's a problem. In Oshmene today there are four thousand Jews. That's twice too many. So, Mr Gens, you've got the whole night. Your police, Dessler in charge –

DESSLER. At your command!

KITTEL. – will go to Oshmene and select half the population. Of course we could send our own men, or, indeed, Lithuanians. What would come of it? Panic. What good would that do? Your people speak Yiddish. If people understand each other they stay calm, everything happens smoothly, efficiently. Police!

The Jewish officers stand. They are half or fully naked.

Well, you're getting new uniforms anyway. In honour of the Oshmene campaign! Russian boots, leather coats, hats once worn by officers of the Czar. Uniforms!

A German officer brings in some uniforms. While the Jewish police put them on, GENS *and* KITTEL *confer.*

GENS. Half the population? They can't all be non-productive.

KITTEL. They can't?

GENS. Impossible. In our experience it's never more than twenty-five per cent.

KITTEL. Gens, I want you to be happy. Let them select only twenty-five per cent.

GENS. On the other hand, if we held a census, it might turn out there were only eight hundred non-productives.

KITTEL. 'Non-productive.' It's relative! You Jews, you'd argue for some eighty year old. Attach a dynamo to his wheelchair, he'll generate power wheeling himself to the toilet.

GENS. No. Age is an absolute. Anyone over eighty, no arguments.

KITTEL. Seventy?

GENS. It's a deal.

KITTEL. But not less than seven hundred people.

GENS. Not less than five hundred, not more than seven.

KITTEL. What's a hundred more or less between friends? Six hundred. What do you say?

GENS. Done!

KITTEL *turns to the policemen who have finished dressing and picked up their clubs.*

KITTEL. Eight Lithuanians from the Ipatinga militia will go with you. Everyone over seventy, pick them out, hand them over to them. Dessler!

DESSLER. Sir! Right face! Forward march! Left right left, left right left . . .

As the police march, everyone leaves except GENS.

GENS. Dessler!

DESSLER *comes back.*

What you're about to do, it's unspeakable. So try not to drool, at least in front of them.

DESSLER. If my heart breaks will I get into heaven? Nor will you. I'm going on your orders. Don't preach to me.

He goes. GENS *spits after him.*

GENS. Scum! (*He drinks.*)

KRUK *enters. For once his typewriter is silent.*

KRUK. They made the selection. Four hundred and ten old and sick Jews were lined up in the square. An old man recited a prayer for the dead, '*El Maleh Rahamim*'. Everyone started crying. Some of the Jewish police who had made the selection broke down and wept. The four hundred and ten were driven in a cart a distance of eight kilometres. When they arrived, the Lithuanians took charge of the execution in the presence of the Jews Dessler, Nathan Ring and Moshe Levas, all three armed with pistols. During the selection, they and the Lithuanians had emptied over one hundred bottles. They roasted a lamb, a gift of the Jewish Council, ate it, went home. Inhabitants of the ghetto lined the streets. Unmoving, unblinking, they watched them go. One of our police, Mr Drazin, started to sing:
   'We came to warm your heart.
   Good night. We now depart.'
While engaged in this massacre, Isaac Averbuch, another policeman, had a nervous collapse and had to be treated by a doctor.

GENS, *drunk, stands.*

GENS. Hermann Kruk is an honest man. And a brave one. Who among us dares to say what he says, even wants to hear the things he dares to talk about? Almost no one. But there are more than a few of us who inside feel as he feels.

More than a few of you consider me a traitor. And you're wondering how it is that I'm still here among you with your innocent, your unsullied souls. I, Jacob Gens, who gives orders to blow up the hideouts you prepare. The same Jacob Gens who puzzles out way after way to save the lives of Jews.

I calculate in Jewish blood not Jewish dignity. The Germans

want a thousand Jews. I hand them over. If I don't, they'll come here and take them by force. And then they won't take a thousand. They'll take thousands. And thousands.

You with your morality. There's dirt, there's filth, you look away. If you survive you'll show your hands – clean. Whereas I, Jacob Gens, will be, if I am anything, drenched in blood, dripping with slime.

I'll submit myself to Jewish justice! I will stand trial! I'll tell them: what I did was done to save Jews, as many as possible, to lead them to freedom. To do this I had no choice but to lead some to death. With my own hands I did it. For the sake of your clean conscience I plunged into filth. I couldn't afford a clean conscience. Could I?

Scene Seventeen

KRUK's *library.* HAYYAH *is searching among the books.* KRUK *comes in.*

KRUK. Can I help?

HAYYAH. I can manage.

KRUK. I've noticed you.

HAYYAH. Yes?

KRUK. You come every day, spend hours searching the shelves. You're not browsing. You're looking for something special.

HAYYAH. Just something to read.

KRUK. I've seen you.

HAYYAH. In the street.

KRUK. I think in the theatre.

HAYYAH. It's possible we've met in the theatre.

KRUK. You perform in revues. Am I wrong?

HAYYAH. I play small parts.

KRUK. You're ashamed of being an actress?

HAYYAH. No. But not proud.

KRUK. Why?

HAYYAH. What's the point of it? For us?

KRUK. I used to feel the same. Now I can see I was wrong.
Fascism turns human beings into animals and uses them for its
own ends. How to resist? Preserve your culture, stay human.
Look, they banned flowers from the ghetto. What did we do?
We gave each other autumn leaves, the most beautiful flowers
in the world.

Silence.

Books on the theatre? Let me see.

HAYYAH (*produces a newspaper*). Look. (*Reads:*) 'The young actor
Gabriel Geivish need only improve his diction, and he is sure if
a successful future on the stage.' *Ghetto News*, 20th March 1943.
Where is he now? . . . 'Diction!' (*She throws away the newspaper.*) I
want a chemistry text book. Something simple.

KRUK *smiles.*

KRUK. Why didn't you say days ago?

He climbs a tall ladder, finds a thin pamphlet.

HAYYAH. Is it in Russian?

KRUK. It's a Soviet army manual. I found it in the library of
technology at the university.

He climbs down the ladder, gives it to her.

The only book I ever stole in my life.

HAYYAH. I can't read it.

KRUK. I'm sure one of your new friends can.

HAYYAH. I'll return it.

KRUK. My eyes are closed. Take it, go. To steal from a thief isn't
stealing.

HAYYAH. Thank you. (*She starts to go.*)

KRUK. Wait!

He takes two or three other books from the shelf and gives them to her.

In case you're stopped.

She kisses him on the cheek and, going, sings the lullaby 'Birds are sleeping on the branches'.

SONG NUMBER TWELVE.

Scene Eighteen

KRUK *remains among his books.* HAYYAH*'s singing is interrupted by a powerful flashlight shone into her face. She freezes. It is* KITTEL.

KITTEL. I can't believe it. Still singing!

HAYYAH. We're rehearsing a new programme.

KITTEL. Your singing at the party was *magnifique.*

He takes the books from her, glances at them.

Russian?

HAYYAH. Can you speak it?

KITTEL. *Nyet! (He laughs.)* Is it a play?

HAYYAH. 'Man Under the Bridge.'

KITTEL. So you'll have it translated?

HAYYAH. Of course.

She reaches for the books. He holds on to them.

KITTEL. Excellent. So you're dancing through the war with a song in your heart.

HAYYAH. When I'm happy, I laugh. When I'm sad, I sing.

KITTEL *(laughing).* A perfect answer. *(He gives her the books.)* When the war is over, perhaps we'll perform together. We'll be quite a double act.

HAYYAH. Wait until you see my next performance.

KITTEL. This time you'll pay off your whole debt, I'm certain.

HAYYAH. I hope so. *(She hurries off.)*

KITTEL. What strange people. *Extraordinaire . . .*

He goes.

Scene Nineteen

KRUK *is in the library.* KITTEL *enters, puts on his black horn-rimmed glasses, becomes* DR PAUL, *enters the library, meets* KRUK.

PAUL. I've brought you a new task. Here is a list of all the monasteries in Vilna. I want you to catalogue their libraries.

KRUK. What for?

PAUL. I'll supervise you. I am trying to protect you. As long as you work for me you're safe.

KRUK. My life means nothing.

PAUL. No? With our eastern front crumbling? The Russians will be here within weeks.

KRUK is excited by the news but pretends indifference so as to squeeze out more information.

KRUK. Within weeks? No, we've heard that before. The war goes on. I haven't the strength for your work. Within weeks! (*He laughs.*)

PAUL. Listen to me. To hold back the Russians, our army is sending non-combatant officers to the front.

KRUK. Aren't you keen to join your friends? This stupid job will keep you here.

Silence.

PAUL. We are both intelligent people. You do this job, I supervise you. Is that clear? Besides, I have authorization from Berlin.

KRUK. No. No, sir. You murderers! You killed my wife, my sister. My mother! You slaughtered my whole family. You want me to save you?

PAUL. Mr Kruk, there is an armed underground in this ghetto. I know that. You have close connections with them. I know that. Think again before you refuse me.

KRUK. An underground? Are you crazy? You conquered the whole of Europe in weeks. How can we, isolated, starved, unarmed in a small defeated ghetto, hope to resist you? No, honestly, we are too clever to even try that.

PAUL. You really stretch out your neck.

KRUK. Kill me. Do it now. I don't care. Kill another thousand – ten thousand! It'll work out the same.

PAUL. What do you mean?

KRUK. The ending was determined long ago. When you fools fired your first shot on Russian soil you wrote the last act. You will play it to the very last line.

PAUL. Which is?

KRUK. 'I will send a fire which will devour palaces. Then the king shall go into captivity, he and his princes together. Your cities will be burned, your people dispersed, driven into exile, scattered over the face of the earth. So saith the Lord.'

PAUL *laughs.*

PAUL. A world ruled by God. Divine justice. Wishful thinking. Who is there to punish us, destroy us, scatter our people?

KRUK. The civilized nations.

PAUL *laughs.*

PAUL. The civilized nations have persecuted you for two thousand years. Who's lost his country? Who's been sent into exile for killing Jews? Believe me, Mr Kruk, the only difference between us and the rest of Europe is that we actually do what they only dream.

KRUK. Speculate all you like. Nothing can justify your crimes.

PAUL. It's speculation? Then why don't the Allies bomb the camps? Do you think they don't know what we're doing? Face reality. You are alone. No one cares about you. The world is ruled by men, by pure naked interest. When the war's over they'll need us, our technology. And the rest? Quickly forgotten.

KRUK. We'll see.

PAUL. Yes, we will. But in order that we do, we must survive. So – the monasteries, their libraries. You work, I supervise.

KRUK *nods.*

And afterwards, if our scientific and spiritual collaboration can continue, I'll be honoured. We have a great deal to offer each other, now and in the future. Goodbye.

PAUL *goes. As* KRUK *dictates, the typewriter is heard in the background.*

KRUK. A new factory for mirrors has been opened at nineteen Rudntizka Street. Another has been started for grindstones, a third produces combs. The technochemical laboratory is being expanded. The bookbinders have spread onto two floors. The sewing workshop grows every day. Two hundred miles from Vilna stands the Red Army, the German sword dangles over our necks, we carry on building our tower of Babel. Will the Russians come in time? Will we survive longer than our enemies? More than ever I cling to my chronicle, my diary, the hashish of my life in the ghetto . . .

Scene Twenty

May Day in the ghetto. Members of the underground resistance rush across and decorate the stage with large red paper flowers, red flags, red banners reading: 'Spring in the Ghetto' and 'May Day – Hurrah!' and 'Yesterday nothing, tomorrow the world!' As they go off, the band enters playing. HAYYAH sings a song of the resistance, others dance. They wear white or dark blue shirts and red scarves.

SONG NUMBER THIRTEEN.

HAYYAH. Yesterday Zalman Tiktin, a young member of the resistance, was shot trying to steal weapons. At this very moment he's lying in the Lukishki Prison Hospital wrestling with death. He is not yet eighteen.

KRUK. At this moment while we celebrate May Day, our brothers in Warsaw are fighting. Fierce fires are burning! The day will come when we too stand up, guns in our hands. Warsaw will be our example! We'll resist to the last man!

SONG NUMBER FOURTEEN.

GENS *rushes in.*

GENS. Stop it! Stop playing!

The music and singing stop.

Where do you think you are? You put the whole ghetto in danger. If they hear that song –

KRUK. You ordered them to start this theatre.

GENS. Not to rub salt in our wounds! Not to spark off rebellion! Listen to me. At long last, things have calmed down. You've never been safer. Why provoke them? Put on plays. Let's have satires. Make them bite. Attack the parasites who won't work. They're the ones who make trouble. But to call our Jewish police traitors? We will lead the ghetto to freedom, not you idiots who spout politics.

KRUK. Mr Gens –

GENS. I forbid you to argue with me. Who in this ghetto has genuine national feeling? Me. Who's the real Jewish patriot? Me. From tomorrow we're going to talk Hebrew. It will be taught in the schools. The bible in Yiddish. An abomination. Hebrew! In junior schools, in nurseries. We'll teach Palestinography! Is anything wrong? I'll tell you what's wrong. There's too little nationalism in Vilna. (*To* SRULIK:) Put on Hebrew plays. I want Hebrew recitations. A blue and white evening, the poems of Bialik. Any actor who rejects the national line is out on his ear.

KRUK. You're learning fast.

GENS. What did you say?

KRUK. Nationalism breeds nationalism.

GENS. This meeting is over. Everyone home!

Everyone goes except SRULIK, *the* DUMMY *and* HAYYAH *who stands alone.* KRUK *returns to his library.*

DUMMY. Hurry! No time to spare. Hurry home, study Hebrew.

SRULIK. Leave me out of it.

DUMMY. It's a famous moment in history. Hurry home, study Hebrew.

SRULIK. I'm too upset for your nonsense.

DUMMY. You call Hebrew nonsense? Mr Gens!

SRULIK. And you? You can't speak a word of it.

DUMMY. I can.

SRULIK. Go on then.

DUMMY. Palestinography.

SRULIK. That isn't Hebrew.

DUMMY. Then what is it? Hurry home, study Hebrew.

HAYYAH *comes to* SRULIK.

HAYYAH. I'm leaving.

DUMMY. And going where? Palestine? (*To* SRULIK:) Let's go with her. Hurry home, study Palestinography.

HAYYAH. This isn't a joke! The Russians aren't far away. Everyone knows that. It's time. I'm joining the underground, leaving tonight through a sewage duct. Will you come?

DUMMY. Your chance to be a hero! She'll fall at your feet! Take me to a sewage duct! Where is the lavatory?

HAYYAH (*to* SRULIK). Will you never be serious?

SRULIK. You know what I think. You want to go? Go. We'll pay the price.

HAYYAH. Not if everyone comes!

SRULIK. How can they? People have families! Grandparents, children. How can they go?

DUMMY. Maybe she's fallen for one of the partisans.

SRULIK. I'm staying.

SRULIK *and* HAYYAH *look at each other, then they embrace.*

DUMMY. At last! She's playing grand opera. But who'll die in the last act?

As HAYYAH *goes, the* DUMMY's *mood changes.*

Hayyah'leh! Don't leave us! Don't leave me! Hayyah'leh!

SRULIK *and the* DUMMY *go off.* OOMA *appears from the dark and addresses* SRULIK.

OOMA. Finita la commedia.

The weight of this sad time we must obey.
Speak what we feel not what we ought to say.
Make all our trumpets speak
Give them all breath
We cannot shape our life
Let's shape our death.

SRULIK *the* DUMMY *and* OOMA *go out.*

Scene Twenty-one

GENS *enters with* WEISKOPF.

GENS. This hall is thirty metres by twenty-five. Almost a thousand metres square. You need two square metres for each sewing machine. Am I right?

WEISKOPF. But this is your theatre!

GENS. I'm finished with that. As a theatre it can save only forty families. You can put five hundred sewing machines here.

WEISKOPF. But what do I need them for? Five hundred more workers? Mr Gens –

GENS. You're about to receive four hundred carloads of uniforms. We'll get a licence for another workshop, no question.

WEISKOPF. I don't need another workshop!

GENS. The Soviet army will be here by December. My duty is to meet them with as many survivors as possible.

WEISKOPF. Listen, squeeze fifty more workers into the old workshop, fifty, I'll polish off those carloads like that.

GENS. You're wrong.

WEISKOPF. I worked it all out.

GENS. Then you worked it out wrong.

WEISKOPF. Mr Gens, this is Weiskopf. You know how long this wise kopf's been in business? Worked it out wrong?

He pulls out a large sheet of paper.

GENS. What's this?

WEISKOPF. My plan. One worker's productivity rate: so and so. See what I mean? Simply add two hours to the working day, then add fifty workers – are you following? – multiply, you get the output. Can I honour my contract or can't I?

GENS takes the paper, examines it.

GENS. You're very methodical.

WEISKOPF. I have to be.

GENS *tears up the plan.*

WEISKOPF. What are you doing?

GENS. Wipe your arse with it.

WEISKOPF. What are you saying?

GENS. Be glad it's not stuffed down your throat! All we need is
for Kittel to get hold of this. Employ five hundred workers, you
save five hundred families. Will I never get through to you?

WEISKOPF. What am I? A charity commissioner? I'm a business
man. I guarantee my workers a living which they earn plus a
little extra for me.

GENS. A little extra. You've become a millionaire. And you're
welcome! I'm no socialist. You work, you've got imagination,
you deserve to flourish. But when does success become blood
sucking? Mr Weiskopf? You will open a workshop in this
theatre. You will employ five hundred workers selected by our
labour exchange.

WEISKOPF (*laughing*). So that's what you're up to. You're going to
offload your cripples on me.

GENS. What are you running here? The Olympic Games? It's just
a shitty workshop fixing shitty uniforms for the shitty Nazis.
For that, Jewish cripples are too good, but if it will help save
their lives . . .

WEISKOPF. Don't you dare call my enterprise shitty! It's my life.
It's my soul. It's me! I won't let you destroy it with shitty
philanthropy.

GENS. You start work here tomorrow.

WEISKOPF. I won't do it.

GENS. You refuse?

WEISKOPF. N spells N, O spells O.

GENS. Then I order you. That's that.

WEISKOPF. You know what to do with your orders.

GENS. What's happened? All of a sudden you don't care about
orders?

WEISKOPF. Why should I? You're not in charge.

GENS. No?

WEISKOPF. There's somebody senior.

GENS. You, perhaps?

WEISKOPF. Kittel.

GENS. Weiskopf, you take this to Kittel –

WEISKOPF. Go on! If I do?

GENS. Weiskopf, you take this to Kittel –

(KITTEL *appears out of nowhere and stands between them. He pretends to be surprised.*)

KITTEL. Gens! What's up?

GENS. This is Weiskopf's new workshop.

KITTEL. A new one? Here? But what's wrong with the old one?

GENS. Too small. He needs five hundred more machines.

KITTEL. What are you sewing? Shrouds for every corpse in Europe?

GENS. You arranged four hundred carloads. We have to gear ourselves up.

KITTEL (*to* WEISKOPF). But five hundred?

WEISKOPF. Uh . . . Mr Kittel, sir, you see . . . five hundred . . . I could manage . . . it depends . . . five hundred? No . . . I could do it with . . . possibly . . .

GENS. Don't make promises you can't keep.

KITTEL. So there's disagreement.

WEISKOPF. No . . . different approaches . . . see what I mean? . . . (*He explodes in a coughing fit.*)

KITTEL. What are you hiding, Weiskopf?

WEISKOPF. Me? Of course, nothing.

KITTEL. That's lucky.

WEISKOPF. Even so –

KITTEL. 'Even so'? Is there disagreement? Yes or no?

GENS. No }
WEISKOPF. Yes. } *together*

KITTEL (*grinning*). Well, at least that's clear.
(*Seriously, to* WEISKOPF:) How many workers do you say you
need?

WEISKOPF. Mr Kittel, give or take –

KITTEL. Precisely!

WEISKOPF. Fifty.

KITTEL. Not five hundred?

WEISKOPF *shakes his head.*

KITTEL. So why inspect this barn? (*To* GENS:) What are you up
to?

GENS. He needs five hundred. Believe me.

KITTEL (*to* WEISKOPF). Where's that plan you showed me?

WEISKOPF *points at* GENS. KITTEL *turns to him.*

GENS. I tore it up. It was a fantasy, a crazy delusion. Look at
him, puffed up with importance, thinks he can fool anyone. It
was a bad joke.

KITTEL (*to* WEISKOPF). You wasted my morning with a trick?

WEISKOPF. Mr Kittel, I swear on the lives of my children . . .
Listen, if you extend the working day by two hours, if you let
me choose my own fifty workers, if –

KITTEL. If and if and if. Three so far.

WEISKOPF. If I can do my own planning –

KITTEL. Four.

WEISKOPF. If no-one interferes –

KITTEL. The next is your last. If you see what I mean.

WEISKOPF. If I could only meet Göring.

KITTEL. If I couldn't see who's talking I'd think it was that doll
with the tongue. But *his* impudence made me smile.

WEISKOPF. If I may remind you, you promised a meeting with
Göring.

KITTEL. What kind of Jew are you? Don't you recognize a joke? People without humour, I hate them.

WEISKOPF. Mr Kittel! I swear! Fifty more workers! I'll get the job done!

KITTEL. Now he's hysterical.

WEISKOPF. I'll make a new plan, I'll work it all out again –

KITTEL. Gens says: no go.

WEISKOPF. But he's head of the ghetto . . .

KITTEL. So?

WEISKOPF. Everyone has their own reasons . . .

KITTEL. You're running with sweat.

WEISKOPF. If I am –

KITTEL. If!

WEISKOPF. Sorry, sorry. Only, please, if you'd . . . sorry . . .

> DESSLER *enters holding a bottle of cognac and a salami.*

DESSLER. Sir!

GENS. Yes?

DESSLER. These were found under Weiskopf's bed.

> KITTEL *takes them.*

KITTEL. French cognac, Hungarian salami. Where were they bought? Weiskopf?

DESSLER. Also half a bag of sugar, ten kilos of rice, five litres of olive oil.

WEISKOPF. These are leftovers from the ball.

KITTEL. God, I love it when people apologise. More!

> WEISKOPF *grabs* KITTEL.

WEISKOPF. Mr Kittel, I want to explain exactly why he wants the five hundred.

KITTEL (*to* GENS). Get this leech off!

GENS. Dessler.

> DESSLER *slaps* WEISKOPF *across the face.* WEISKOPF *protects his*

face with his hands, freeing KITTEL. *With one swoop,* DESSLER *pulls all the buttons off* WEISKOPF's *trousers. They fall to the floor.* WEISKOPF *pulls them up with both hands. Meantime* DESSLER *has put on the knuckledusters hanging from his belt. As* WEISKOPF *pulls up his trousers,* DESSLER *hits him in the face with the knuckledusters.* WEISKOPF *screams, falls to the ground.* DESSLER *picks him up. His face is running with blood.* DESSLER *hits him again. He falls again and lies still.*

GENS (*to* DESSLER). Lock him up.

DESSLER *lifts up* WEISKOPF, *starts to drag him off. While watching,* KITTEL *has opened the cognac and taken a drink.*

KITTEL (*to* GENS). Congratulations. My prize pupil.

He hands the bottle to GENS *who drinks.*

Call back your baboon.

GENS. Dessler!

DESSLER. Sir!

GENS. Over here!

DESSLER *drops* WEISKOPF, *goes to* GENS.

KITTEL. Call the actors. I can't wait any longer. I want a preview of what they're rehearsing.

DESSLER. Sir!

KITTEL. Now!

DESSLER *does an about-face, picks up* WEISKOPF, *drags him out.*

KITTEL. Something serious. People are escaping from the ghetto.

GENS. That's not possible.

KITTEL. A train was blown up, fifteen German soldiers killed. Forty villagers have paid with their lives. I don't weep for them. They were saints. Their souls are singing where neither yours nor mine ever will. But the truth is, the bomb was made by amateurs. Our experts believe by someone who broke out of here. I did research. In the past two weeks, thirty people have vanished from their work teams. (*He laughs.*) Tell me, Mr Gens, I'm right, am I not, to think you Jews familiar with the doctrine of mutual responsibility? What do your wise men say? 'One hand washes the other.'

GENS. Each Jew is responsible for all others.

KITTEL. I want to try that around here. If anyone disappears, his family will be killed. If a whole family disappears, all who shared their room. If everyone from a room gets away, we dynamite the building. Divide your workers into groups of ten. If one runs off, nine will be slaughtered. Have I interpreted your doctrine correctly? And no new workshops. Weiskopf wasn't lying. I went through his plan in great detail. It was brilliant. So, what will you do now?

Silence.

Speak up.

GENS. Reappoint him.

KITTEL. To do what?

GENS. Run the workshops . . .

KITTEL. Every time I think I've finally penetrated your Jewish brains, I hit a bone wall. And you're supposed to be geniuses. You understand nothing of the world. Gens, there are no second chances. If a person trips, bury him. In the quarrel between you and Weiskopf I was interested only in whose will was stronger. The second he started to sweat it was over. He's a worm. Stamp on him. You played your part like a master. So get on with it. Appoint a new director of the workshops. There's the four hundred carloads and no extra labour. Come on, Gens, don't disappoint me. I've taught you all I know. Where are the actors? I want to see them now.

Scene Twenty-two

Light comes up on stage.
Empty Nazi UNIFORMS *rise out of the pile of clothes. They are bullet-ridden and stained with blood. They assemble as though at a Nazi mass meeting to listen to the Führer who is represented by a* UNIFORM *of the kind Hitler wore when addressing a military parade. This* UNIFORM *is worn by* SRULIK. *The faces and limbs of all the actors are concealed. Only the face of the* DUMMY, *manipulated by* SRULIK, *is visible among all the empty* UNIFORMS. *It wears the same costume as before.*

HITLER UNIFORM. Comrades! Look around you! What do you see?

ALL (*looking around*). What do we see?

HITLER UNIFORM. We're surrounded by Jews!

ALL. By Jews.

HITLER UNIFORM. Go anywhere, look anywhere – nothing but Jews. Turn to the right.

He brings the DUMMY *violently to his right.*

A Jew.

DUMMY. My mother was Aryan.

HITLER UNIFORM. Shut up!

DUMMY. I'm not Jewish! Ask any Rabbi.

HITLER UNIFORM. I decide who is Jewish.

DUMMY. You'll get into trouble.

HITLER UNIFORM. Turn to the left.

He flings the DUMMY *violently to the left.*

Another Jew!

DUMMY. Hey! It's me! I'm the same one!

The HITLER UNIFORM *flings the* DUMMY *in all directions.*

HITLER UNIFORM. And another, and another, yet another! You go to the opera, nothing but Jews. To the theatre, Jews. The concert hall, Jews. The newspapers, the banks, the pimps, the doctors, the lawyers, the dentists. So you start wondering, is this a Jew? Is this a Jew? Is this also a Jew?

ALL (*ad lib.*). Is this a Jew? Is this a Jew!

HITLER UNIFORM. Comrades!

Silence.

We are asking the wrong question. What should we ask?

He pulls up the DUMMY *and displays it to his audience.*

We should ask, is this a German?

All the UNIFORMS *laugh.*

HITLER UNIFORM. You should ask, is this a human being?

UNIFORM 1. How can we know?

HITLER UNIFORM. Good question. Any suggestions?

UNIFORM 2. Can it stand on its legs?

HITLER UNIFORM. Let's find out.

He lets go of the DUMMY. *It collapses in a bundle. The* UNIFORMS *roar with laughter.*

UNIFORM 3. Does it have a backbone?

HITLER UNIFORM. Let's see.

He makes the DUMMY *bend and twist in all directions. Laughter.*

UNIFORM 4. Hath a Jew eyes?

HITLER UNIFORM. Eyes?

The DUMMY *seems to become all eyes, rolling its eyes in all directions, squinting, doing everything to draw attention to its eyes. As the* UNIFORMS *have no eyes of their own they can't see those of the* DUMMY.

Does anyone see eyes?

ALL (*ad lib.*) I can't see anything. I see nothing.

UNIFORM 5. Hath it limbs?

HITLER UNIFORM. Limbs? Does anyone see limbs?

Now the DUMMY *becomes all hands and feet, to no avail.*

UNIFORM 6. Hath it senses, affections, passions?

The DUMMY *acts out its passions, affections, senses as best it can.*

HITLER UNIFORM. It doesn't look like it.

UNIFORM 7. Is a Jew fed with the same food?

UNIFORM 8. No, it drinks our blood.

UNIFORM 9. If you prick it, does it bleed?

HITLER UNIFORM. What an intelligent question. Let's find out.

He stabs the DUMMY, *slashing open its costume. A flood of coins pours out onto the ground. Wild laughter.*

UNIFORM 10. If you tickle it, does it laugh?

HITLER UNIFORM. Everyone, try!

The UNIFORMS *produce whips. They 'tickle' the* DUMMY *with the edges of their whips. The* DUMMY *does its best to produce a laughter-*

like noise. It sounds like suppressed anguish and pain.

UNIFORM 11. One more question. If you poison it, does it die?

HITLER UNIFORM. Bravo! That's *the* question. Let's see.

All the UNIFORMS *produce pre-war DDT pumps and spray the* DUMMY. *Silence. The* DUMMY *is paralysed for a moment, then it starts quivering all over, twisting in all directions, starting its long death agony. The* UNIFORMS *recoil.*

UNIFORM 1. We've done it!

UNIFORM 2. We've done it!

UNIFORM 3. We are rid of this creature who boiled us in boric and chloric.

UNIFORM 4. And wrenched us and drenched us.

UNIFORM 5. And wrung us and hung us.

UNIFORM 6. And starched us.

UNIFORM 7. And ironed us.

ALL. We are finally free of the Jew!

HITLER UNIFORM. Comrades, dear comrades, I proclaim the Kingdom of new freedom. We are free of this blood-sucker. Our freedom will last a thousand years! Musicians, to your instruments. One, two, three –

The HITLER UNIFORM *starts singing Beethoven's 'Ode to Joy' from the Ninth Symphony. All the empty* UNIFORMS *join in the singing while the poisoned* DUMMY *performs its dance of death.*

KITTEL. Bravo! Bravo!

As he applauds he whispers to GENS. GENS *goes out.*

Line up facing me.

The UNIFORMS *form a row facing* KITTEL.

As satire, that was outstanding. And I'm an expert. I used to perform in satirical cabaret in the thirties.

He sings.

'Und wenn dann der Kopf fallt, sage ich:
Hoppla!
Und ein Schiff mit acht Segeln und mit

*funfzig Kanonen wird beschiessen
die Stadt . . .'*

He laughs nostalgically.

Yes, I certainly appreciate satire. I'd like to see the actors.

DUMMY. What actors? We're nothing but uniforms.

KITTEL *(fiercely)*. I asked to see the actors. Hurry up!

Slowly and uncertainly, the faces of the actors emerge from the clothes. First one head, then another. Gradually they all appear. Only one remains empty. KITTEL approaches it.

You too! Let's have a look at you.

KITTEL *looks inside. He is astonished.*

It's empty. But that singer was in there! I heard her voice! How did you do it? What a fantastic piece of staging! She's really not there. Who did the voice for her?

Silence.

(To SRULIK). It must have been you.

DUMMY. It was me! It was me!

KITTEL. A brilliant effect. Magical. Bravo, gentlemen. I let you use watches. Even fountain pens. I allowed the cafés, the symposia on cultural subjects, the orchestra. Above all the theatre! And why? Because you owed me sixty grams of beans! This is how I'm repaid. I asked to see the full company. One actress, who still owes me fifteen grams, has disappeared. Have you heard the new orders concerning people who escape from the ghetto? 'One hand washes the other.' Well, you've dirtied yours. Satire! I'll give you satire! Faces to the wall!

All the actors face the wall.

Machine gunner, over here!

The sound of the squeaking hinges of a cart. The screeching noise is blood curdling. GENS enters pushing a cart. On it is a large pot labelled 'Jam'. Next to the pot is a large basket with a sliced loaf of challah. KITTEL commands:

Position the gun there! Load gun! Ready! *(He himself cocks the Schmeisser.)* Everyone – about turn!

The actors turn round with expressions of horror on their faces. They are astonished to see the jam and the bread. KITTEL *roars with laughter.*

You thought I was going to shoot you. That's so funny! After your marvellous performance? In these very dark days, our armies retreating, the Russians about to break through, you've given me pleasure, real elation, true joy. Your artistry has saved your lives. This expresses my appreciation. A pot full of jam, fine white bread. Help yourselves. (KITTEL *takes bread, dips it in the jam, eats.*) Delicious. It's blackcurrant. Won't you join me?

Hesitantly, the actors approach the pot. Gradually they relax and fall on the food ravenously. They crowd round the pot. As they eat the DUMMY *sings.*

SONG NUMBER FIFTEEN.

After a while, KITTEL *moves away from the actors. He watches them, then lifts his Schmeisser and guns them all down, including* GENS, *in one long round. Only* SRULIK *remains still wearing his uniform, facing* KITTEL *like a mirror image. The* DUMMY *frees itself from* SRULIK's *hold; it advances towards* KITTEL *as an independent person and for the first time sings in its own voice impudently to* KITTEL's *face.*

SONG NUMBER FIFTEEN (*last verse.*)

KITTEL *shoots the* DUMMY. *The* DUMMY *sinks slowly to the ground.* SRULIK's *arm is bullet ridden and torn to shreds. He struggles over the bodies of the dead actors and becomes the old* NARRATOR *from Scene One.*

NARRATOR. Our last performance? Our last performance . . . Wait a moment . . .

End

Songs
Lyrics and music by the inhabitants of the Vilna Ghetto
translated and arranged by Jeremy Sams

Song Number One

UNTER DAINE VAISSE SHTEREN

In the sky the stars all glisten,
Here below I am lost in pain.
When I pray does no-one listen?
Is my weeping all in vain?
As I watch, the stars all darken,
All alone I stand and stare.
Let the empty heavens harken
To my broken-hearted prayer.
Let the empty heavens harken
To my humble prayer.

Take my prayers and take my yearning
These are everything I own.
In my head a fire is burning
But my heart has turned to stone.
Cellars seethe with hell and fire
Streets are paved with black despair.
To the rooftops, climbing, higher,
Father let me find you there.
To the rooftops, ever higher
Let me find you there.

Silent screams are deafening
And moaning ghosts are everywhere.
I am like a broken string
But still I sing my broken prayer.
In the sky the stars still glisten
Lilies in a field of white.

How I pray that God will listen
To my lonely song tonight.
How I pray that He will listen
To my song tonight . . .

Song Number Two

HOT ZICH MIR DI SHICH ZERISSN

Someone stole my overcoat
So how will I keep warm?
Who will hide me from this biting cold
Or shield me from the storm?
So dance with me, and keep the cold away
If you've got your papers you can marry me today.

Every week they change the papers
Red or green or blue.
Every blessed week a different colour
What am I to do?
So dance with me . . . (etc.)

Ask for wood you get a splinter
Ask for bread, a stone.
Ah, this bitter wind, this cruel winter
Chills me to the bone.
So dance with me . . . (etc.)

Song Number Three

VEI ZU DI TEG

(Recit)

Ah my children, my children . . . such times we live in
A curse on the day . . . a curse on the night.

(Song)

It's a time of steel and concrete
A time of murder and machines.
Every night we hear the railways
Won't you tell us what it means?
Just say what you're thinking.
Don't be afraid to tell us what is wrong.
You walk round bewildered
Be silent if you must – but be strong.
Now nothing is right – there's nothing to say
A curse on the night – a curse on the day.

Song Number Four

'Swanee' by George Gershwin. Available from International
Music Publications, Unit 15, Woodford Trading Estate,
Southend Road, Woodford Green, Essex I G8 8HN.

Song Number Five

SHTILER, SHTILER

Go to sleep my little flower don't let them hear you cry,
Graves are growing hour by hour 'til they fill the sky.
Since your father went away the world is wearing black,
Many roads lead to Ponar but none of them lead back.
Hush-a-bye my little treasure – time to go to sleep;
It would only give them pleasure if they heard you weep.
Every prison has a door
And every wave breaks on the shore,
But pain for you and I will never die.

Spring is blooming here today and all the world is bright.
All we see is winter's grey, a cold and endless night.
Even when the flames of autumn flicker from afar
Still the mothers are the orphans – children in Ponar.
Still the river is in chains, still yearning to be free.
It grinds its way through Lithuania 'til it finds the sea,
Let the darkness fade away
And let us see the light of day.
Father come again and end our pain.

Pain is growing slowly here with sorrow all around,
'Til our jailors disappear you may not make a sound.
Do not smile until tomorrow, do not cry today.
You must not betray our sorrow 'til it's died away.
Sorrow's wider than a river, deeper than a well.
Soon your father will deliver you and I from Hell.
Soon the world will loose its chains
And all the flowers will bloom again
And heaven's golden grace will fill your face . . .

Song Number Six

LULLABY

Hush my child, the winds are blowing
Sleep and don't despair.
They took away your father from us
God alone knows where.

Song Number Seven

YIDISHE BRIGADES

Forget the sun – forget the flowers
Forget the rain that's going to fall.
This golden time – it isn't ours
We have the right to work, that's all.

Yidishe Brigade
Working ever harder.
Our wages are blood and sweat.
But we are not defeated yet.
Yidishe Brigade (etc.)

We do not ask for your compassion
A man is proud to be a slave
But all the songs we sing against you
Will carry on beyond the grave
Yidishe Brigade (etc).

We live like beasts inside the Ghetto
You only lead us out to Death
But we will sing and we will curse you
Until we draw our final breath.

Yidishe Brigade
Working ever harder
Our wages are blood and sweat
But we are not defeated yet
Yidishe Brigade
Working ever harder
We're marching hand in hand
Until we reach the promised land

Song Number Eight

ISRULIK

(Refrain)

I'm Isrulik – the orphan of the Ghetto,
I'm Isrulik – the boy the world forgot.
Of all my family there's me remaining.
I'm not complaining, I'm happy with my lot.

Your life is worth a farthing,
Your work's worth even less
So business gets tougher every day.
No wonder we're all starving,
No wonder life's a mess.
You've got to find a way to make it pay.

(Refrain)

I'll flog you golden earrings,
I'll flog you cigarettes,
Or saccharin or bread or currant jam.
If anyone starts jeering,
If anyone forgets,
I'll make sure they remember who I am.

(Refrain)

My mother I've forgotten,
I wouldn't know her face.
They took away my parents long ago.
I'm stuck here in this rotten
And God-forsaken place
It's better if you stick with what you know . . .

(Refrain)

I'm Isrulik and if you watch me closely
You might see me try to wipe my eye
We all have sorrows – so why regret them
You'd best forget them.
They'll only make you cry . . .

(Refrain)

Song Number Nine

FRILING

I walk through the Ghetto alone and forsaken,
There's no-one to care for me now.
And how can you live when your love has been taken,
Will somebody please show me how?
I know that it's springtime, and birdsong, and sunshine,
All nature seems happy and free,
But locked in the Ghetto I stand like a beggar,
I beg for some sunshine for me.

(Refrain)

Springtime, what good is springtime,
What good is sunshine, when he is away?
Springtime, you shine upon my sorrow, but still tomorrow
Is as bleak as today.

The house that we lived in is now barricaded,

The windows are broken and bare.
The sun is so fierce that the flowers have faded,
They wilt in the wintery air.
Each morning, each evening I have to walk past it,
Hiding my eyes from the sight
The place where you loved me the place where you kissed
    me,
The place where you held me so tight.

(Refrain)

How thoughtful, how kind of the heavenly powers
To send spring so early this year.
Why thank you for coming, I see you brought flowers
You want me to welcome you here?
They say that the Ghetto is golden and glowing
But sunlight and tears make me blind.
You see, my beloved, how soon they start flowing
I can't get you out of my mind.

(Refrain)

Song Number Ten

JE T'AIME – C'EST FOU
(lyrics by Joshua Sobol
music by Jeremy Sams)

Je suis peut être mal foutue
Je suis peut être pas normale
Mais j'aime l'amour que me tue
Oui j'aime l'amour qui m'fait mal.

Quand je te vois, ma bete
Je perds ma tete
C'est pas chouette
Mais c'est comme ça

Quand tu me tiens
Mon animal
Je me sens sale
Quand tu me fais mal
Mais c'est comme ça.

Embrasse moi
Tout doux, c'est bon
Embrasse moi
Mon doux amour.

Je t'aime mon choux
Mon beau Teuton
Je t'aime: c'est fou
Comme j'aime ma mort.

Quand tu me caresses
De ton regard
Je suis ta maitresse
N'est pas bizarre –
Que quand je te vois dans mes rêves
C'est drôle, mais je te vois qui crêve.

Quand je te vois ma bête
Je perds la tête.
C'est pas chouette
Mais c'est comme ça.

Quand tu me tiens
Mon animal
Je me sens sale
Quand tu m'fais mal
Mais c'est comme ça.

Embrasse moi
Tout doux, c'est bon
Embrasse moi
Mon doux amour

Je rêve des nuits
Je rêve des jours
Ou je serais ta veuve
Je la serais toujours, toujours, toujours

Song Number Eleven

MIR LEBN EIBIK

We'll live for ever – year after year.
We'll live for ever, for we are here.
And if they try to drag our names through the mud,

We will rewrite them in our enemy's blood.
We'll live forever – beyond the flames
And you will never forget our names.
So we will fight and we will strive, to carry on, to stay alive.
We'll live forever. We will survive.

Song Number Twelve

DREMLEN FEIGL

Birds are dreaming in the treetops,
Stars are in the sky.
Who's the stranger by your bedside
Singing you a lullaby?
Liu, liu . . .

All our love lies cradled with you,
Shielding you from pain;
For your mother, your poor mother
Won't be coming back again . . .
Liu liu . . .

And I saw your father running
In a hail of stones
All our God-forsaken country
Echoes to his moans
Liu liu. . . .

Song Number Thirteen

MAYDAY SONG

We've dragged through the mud
And we're swimming in blood
Our bodies can't take any more
So stand and unite – move into the light
You see how our people betray us.
Don't waste your despair

On weeping and prayer.
The heavens are empty there's nobody there.
So stand and unite
Move into the light.
You see how our people betray us
So fight!

Song Number Fourteen

ZOG NIT KEINMOL

Never say the final journey is at hand
Never say we will not reach the promised land.
Never doubt the day of reckoning is near.
There's a drumming in the land – and we are here.
From the land of palm-trees to the land of snow.
We are marching we are singing as we go
And each and every drop of Jewish blood to fall
Will be tribute to the courage of us all.
Our tomorrows will be bathed in golden light
And our enemies will vanish with the night,
And we know that perfect morning won't be long,
When every generation sings this song
It's a song that's from the fields and from the flood.
It's a song that's tipped in steel and dipped in blood.
It's a song that's of our people and our land.
It's a song that has a sickle in its hand.
Do not falter . . . (etc.)

Song Number Fifteen

PAK ZICH AIN

Move along, move along,
Every Jew knows this song.
Every year they sing it for us.
All the world joins in the chorus,
Move along, move along.

Move along, move along,
Pack your bags, join the throng.
Come on, change your life, resettle,
Leave your wife, leave the shtetl,
Move along, move along.

Move along, move along,
Earthly life won't last long
But even faced with Heaven's glory,
It will be the same old story
Move along, move along.

UNTER DAINE VAISSE SHTEREN

Moderato

In the sky the stars all glis-ten Here be-low I am
lost in pain when I pray does no-one listen?
Is my weep-ing all in vain? As I watch, the stars all dar-ken
All a-lone I stand and stare Let the emp-ty hea-vens har-ken
To my bro-ken-heart-ed prayer Let the emp-ty
hea-vens har-ken To my hum-ble prayer.

HOT ZICH MIR DI SHICH ZERISSN

Some-one stole my ov-er-coat So how will I keep
warm who will hide me from this bit-ing cold Or
shield me from the storm So dance with me, and
keep the cold a - way   If   you've got your
pa - pers you can mar - ry me to-day So
dance with me   and   keep the cold a -
way   If   you've got your pa - pers you can
mar - ry me to - day

VEI ZU DI TEG

It's a time of steel and con-crete
A

time of mur-der and ma-chines

Eve-ry night we hear the rail-ways

Won't you tell us what it means Just

say what you've think-ing Don't

be a-fraid to tell us what is wrong You

walk a-round be-wild-ered Be

sil-ent it you have to but be strong Now

no-thing is right - and there's no-thing to say
A

curse on the night - a curse on the day Now

SHTILER, SHTILER

Andante

Go to sleep my lit-tle flower don't let them hear you cry

Graves are grow-ing hour by hour 'til they fill the sky

Since your fa-ther went a-way the world is wear-ing black

Ma-ny roads lead to Po-nar but none of them lead back

Hush-a-bye my lit-tle trea-sure — time to go to sleep

It would on-ly give them plea-sure if they heard you weep

Eve-ry pri-son has a door And eve-ry wave breaks

on the shore But pain for you and I will ne-ver die.

LULLABY

Hush my child, the winds are blow - ing
Sleep and don't des - pair. They
took a - way your fath - er from us
God a - lone knows where.

YIDISHE BRIGADES

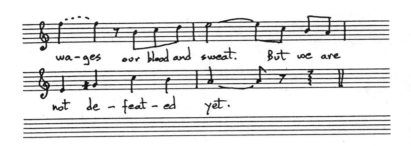

wa-ges   our blood and sweat.   But we are

not de - feat - ed   yet.

ISRULIK

Con Moto

I'm Is-ru-lik the or-phan of the Ghet-to
I'm Is-ru-lik the boy the world for-got Of
all my fami-ly there's me re-main-ing I'm
not com-plain-ing, I'm hap-py with my lot.
Your life is worth a far-thing Your
work's worth ev-en less So bus-i-ness gets
tough-er eve-ry day No won-der we've all
star-ving No won-der life's a mess You've
got to find a way to make it pay

FRILING

I walk through the Ghetto a-lone and for-sa-ken There's
no-one to care for me now   Ah
how can you live when your love has been ta-ken Will
some-bo-dy please show me how?   I
know that its spring-time, and bird-song, and sun-shine All
na-ture seems hap-py and free   But
locked in the Ghet-to I stand like a beg-gar I
beg for some sun-shine for me   Spring-time,
what good is spring-time   what good is

son-shine when he is a-way
spring-time you shine u-pon my sor-row
but still to-mor-row Is as bleak as today day.

JE T'AIME – C'EST FOU
(lyrics by Joshua Sobol
music by Jeremy Sams)

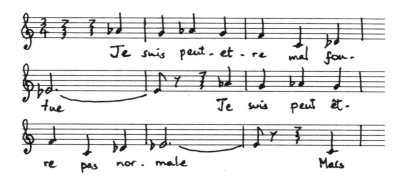

Je suis peut-et-re mal foutue Je suis peut êt-
re pas nor-male Mais

bon Em - brass - e moi Mon

doux a - mour Je t'aime mon

choux mon beau Teu - ton Je

t'aime: c'est fou - com-me

j'ai-me ma mort

Quand tu me car-

resses de ton re - gard je

suis ta maî-tresse n'est pas bi-zarre

Que quand je te vois dans mes

rêves C'est drôle, mais je

te vois qui crève

Quand je te vois ma bê te

MIR LEBN EIBIK

We'll live for ev-er year af-ter year. We'll live for
ev-er, for we are here And if they try to
drag our names through the mud We will rewrite them in oor en-e-my's blood We'll live for
ev-er be-yond the flames And you will ne-ver
for-get oor names And we will fight and we will
strive, to car-ry on, to stay a-live We'll live for
ev-er We will sur-vive.

DREMLEN FEIGL

Birds are dream-ing in the tree-tops

Stars are in the sky

Who's the stran-ger by your bed - side

Sing-ing you a lull-a - by?

Who's the stran-ger by your bed - side

Sing-ing you a lull-a - by?   Liv,

liv,   Liv, liv,   liv.

MAYDAY SONG

We're dragged through the mud And we're swim-ming in blood Our
bod-ies can't take an-y more. So
stand and u-nite — move in-to the light You
see how our peo-ple be-tray us. Don't
waste your des-pair On weep-ing and prayer The
hea-vens are emp-ty there's no-bo-dy there So
stand and u-nite Move in-to the light. You
see how our peo-ple be-tray us So
fight!

ZOG NIT KEINMOL

Never say the final journey is at hand Never say we will not reach the promised land, Never doubt the day of reckoning is near There's a drumming in the land — and we are here.

PAK ZICH AIN

Move along, move along Every Jew knows this song. Every year they sing it for us All the world joins in the chorus Move along, move along